IMAGES OF WAR

THE FRENCH AIR FORCE IN THE FIRST WORLD WAR

RARE PHOTOGRAPHS FROM WARTIME ARCHIVES

Ian Sumner

Pen & Sword
AVIATION

First published in Great Britain in 2018 by
PEN & SWORD AVIATION
An imprint of
Pen & Sword Books Ltd
47 Church Street
Barnsley
South Yorkshire
S70 2AS

ISBN 978-1-52670-179-4

Typeset by Concept, Huddersfield, West Yorkshire HD4 5JL.
Printed and bound in England by CPI Group (UK) Ltd, Croydon CR0 4YY.

Pen & Sword Books Limited incorporates the imprints of Atlas, Archaeology, Aviation, Discovery, Family History, Fiction, History, Maritime, Military, Military Classics, Politics, Select, Transport, True Crime, Air World, Frontline Publishing, Leo Cooper, Remember When, Seaforth Publishing, The Praetorian Press, Wharncliffe Local History, Wharncliffe Transport, Wharncliffe True Crime and White Owl.

For a complete list of Pen & Sword titles please contact
PEN & SWORD BOOKS LIMITED
47 Church Street, Barnsley, South Yorkshire S70 2AS, England
E-mail: enquiries@pen-and-sword.co.uk
Website: www.pen-and-sword.co.uk

Contents

Introduction

When Orville and Wilbur Wright made their pioneering flight in 1903, soldiers and politicians were quick to embrace the military potential of the new technology. Over the next decade aircraft developed rapidly in power and speed, while armies tackled the challenge of creating an aviation service, positioning it within the existing chain of command and evolving a doctrine to govern its use. None of the warring powers had resolved these issues by August 1914, but the subsequent four years of conflict served as a spur to rapid evolution. French aircraft became integral to the ultimate Allied victory, laying the basis for operational developments such as fighters, strategic bombing and photo-reconnaissance later to become standard in the Second World War.

The images presented here do not offer an illustrated chronology. Rather, they seek to capture the men and machines of the new service and their experience of the novel world of aerial conflict, complementing my earlier *Kings of the Air: French Aces and Airmen in the Great War* (Pen & Sword, 2015), which pursues the same themes and personalities in greater depth. Chapter 1 covers the pre-war creation of the service, its deployment in 1914, and the training of pilots and ground crew through-out the conflict. Chapter 2 tackles reconnaissance and artillery spotting, the roles originally envisaged for aircraft as a replacement for static balloons; in practice, old and new technologies complemented each other, and both are discussed here. Chapter 3 features bombing, quickly identified as a means of carrying the war to the enemy, whether by dirigible balloon or increasingly by aircraft. Chapter 4 explores air-to-air combat and the struggle to develop and deploy an effective fighter type. Chapter 5 examines the defence of Paris, while Chapter 6 looks at the relationship between the new arm of service and the vociferous lobbyists of the fast-developing air-craft industry. Chapter 7 concludes by considering the final year of the war and the strategic, tactical and technical developments that transformed aircraft into such a powerful tool for Allied commanders.

The basic unit within the aviation service was the squadron (*escadrille*), consisting of six aircraft in 1914, ten in 1916, and fifteen in 1917. Each squadron was numbered sequentially on its creation, although several renumberings took place during the war and some units underwent more than one redesignation. Each number was also allocated an alphabetical prefix to indicate the main aircraft type operated by the squadron. A single squadron might operate under a series of different prefixes – for example, 3rd Squadron was designated successively BL3, MS3, N3 and SPA3, reflecting its re-equipment with Blériot, Morane-Saulnier, Nieuport and SPAD types. Usage was never standardized: SPAD squadrons, for example, were prefixed S, Sp or SPA. The principal designations used here are: BR (Breguet), C (Caudron), D (Deperdussin), DO (Dorand), MF (Maurice Farman), MS (Morane-Saulnier), N (Nieuport), SPA (SPAD), or V (Voisin).

In the early days of the war, each squadron acted independently, reporting to an army or army corps commander. As the conflict progressed, however, the squadrons were combined in larger formations – initially provisional *groupements* or permanent *groupes*. In December 1914, a number of bomber squadrons were combined to form *Groupes de Bombardement* (GB), each three or four squadrons strong. From the spring of 1916, a number of fighter squadrons were placed in ad hoc *groupements* to meet the needs of a particular operation or tactical situation, and in November 1916 permanent fighter *groupes* were created, described either as *Groupes de Combat* or *Groupes de Chasse* (GC). Over the next year or so, the *groupes* were combined from time to time in provisional *groupements* under a single commander, as the local situation required. In February 1918, *escadres* were created as still larger formations: the *Escadres de Bombardement* (EB), each comprising three bomber *groupes*, and the *Escadres de Combat* (EC), each comprising four fighter *groupes*. In May 1918, two fighter *escadres* and two bomber *escadres*, plus a reconnaissance *groupe*, were combined to form the Air Division. The division contained a variable number of *escadres*, according to operational need. One fighter *escadre* and one bomber *escadre* were often placed under a single command as a 'brigade'.

Acknowledgements

My thanks go to all who have helped in writing this book. The collections of the Service Historique de la Défense at Vincennes, the Bibliothèque Nationale, Archives Nationales and École Nationale Supérieure des Beaux-Arts in Paris, the Musée de l'Air et de l'Espace at Le Bourget, and the British Library in London have all provided a wealth of research material. So too have Albin Denis and Claude Thollon-Pomerol, whose tireless work has contributed so much to the history of French military aviation during the First World War. Finally, the finished work would be nothing without the translating and editing skills of my wife Margaret, to whom I remain hugely indebted.

Most of the images included here are drawn from the collections of the Bibliothèque de Documentation Internationale Contemporaine (BDIC) at the Université Paris Nanterre. I am grateful to its staff and to the following individual photographers:

Bertaux: 21 (bottom), 22, 125
Boisseaux: 47 (top), 58 (bottom), 78
Bonnemaison: 37
Boucaud: 82
Boucher: 112
Brauger: 81
Camondo: 50, 51 (both), 54 (bottom)
Castex: 27 (top), 124 (top)
Charpentier: 101 (bottom)
Couturier: 40

Fleury: 93
Guidan : 124 (bottom)
d'Hauteserve: 79 (bottom)
Lapeyre: 58 (top), 91 (bottom), 94, 95 (top)
Martin: 148
de Preissac: 62 (bottom), 63, 102 (bottom)
Royer: 41 (top)
Ruyssen: 90

The image on 152 (bottom) comes from the NYPL Digital Collection.

Every effort has been made to avoid infringements of copyright and all omissions are unintentional. If this has occurred, please contact the publisher who will include the appropriate credit in future printings and editions.

Chapter One

'. . . difficult, dangerous, at times impossible'

After a decade of hectic development, the French air service was able to take the field in August 1914 with a substantial force of 132 aircraft divided between twenty-five squadrons. Numbers, however, told only half the story. The early years of the service had been, and still were, bedevilled by controversy, as engineers and artillery disputed the purpose of the new machines and vied for their control.

Already responsible for military ballooning, the engineers were first out of the blocks, making an abortive trip to Ohio in 1906 to negotiate the purchase of several Wright *Flyers*. By then, however, French manufacturers were also up and running, offering machines more powerful and stable than their American counterparts and equipped with wheels instead of skids. In August 1909, at Bétheny (Marne), the first international air meeting attracted a wide range of planes and pilots, as well as huge crowds of enthusiastic onlookers. Among them were a group of army officers, there to evaluate the machines on show, and within weeks five planes had been purchased for the engineers to create a military aviation service. The artillery fought back at once: the obvious purpose of the new technology, they argued, was spotting for the guns. In response, a separate artillery aviation section was created at Vincennes, where a research team soon began to investigate all aspects of military flying: shell-spotting, reconnaissance, bombing and armament.

From 1910 the new machines took part in the annual autumn manoeuvres, demonstrating their value in reconnaissance and shell-spotting, as well as the benefits of equipping each squadron with a single aircraft type. The aircraft themselves, however, remained embryonic. A competition in September 1911 promised huge cash prizes and guaranteed government orders to the winners, but only sixteen of the seventy-one entrants survived the preliminary round. Engines as yet lacked the power to lift the specified 300kg load, and the final rankings were determined largely by speed. Heavy and hard to handle, most soon proved unfit for active service.

In 1912, the air service was formally recognized as a branch of the engineers, and the following year it joined the balloon service to form a fifth department within the army, equal in status to the infantry, cavalry, engineers and artillery. Yet the inter-departmental conflict continued to rage, and in August 1913 the artillery gained the upper hand. General Félix Bernard, the first director of aviation, was a gunner utterly blind to his new command. Aircraft, he opined, were useful only for shell-spotting 'whenever telegraph wires prevent the raising of a captive balloon'. In his ignorance and mistrust of the new machines, however, Bernard was only too typical of his peers. Just a handful of senior officers had any experience of working with aircraft, and when the Germans invaded in August 1914 few commanders were prepared to trust the intelligence gathered by the many French reconnaissance missions flown.

Later that month, with the enemy nearing Paris, one crew spotted the German First Army change its direction of march — but the corps commander simply refused to believe them. Only when the information reached General Joseph Gallieni, commander of the Paris garrison — the Camp Retranché de Paris (CRP) — did it provoke a reaction, allowing the French to halt the invader on the Marne. Nor, in the confusion of the retreat, did aircraft have much opportunity to contribute as shell-spotters. Air combat, however, soon featured. Pilots and observers started to carry personal weapons straight away — in self-defence as well as to cripple their opponents — and on 5 October 1914, flying a Voisin 3 equipped with a jury-rigged machine gun, pilot Joseph Frantz (V24) and observer Louis Quenault shot down an enemy aircraft, recording the first confirmed victory in air-to-air combat.

Struggling to find a role, the air service was also desperately short of personnel. Confident the war would be short and pilots unnecessary, in August 1914 the hapless Bernard had closed the military flying schools and returned all current trainees to their regiments. Within weeks the army was scouring its ranks for volunteer aircrew, ideally men with a technical background, although in 1915 many former cavalry officers also transferred successfully. The pre-war schools were reopened and new schools added. Here aspiring pilots earned their wings, attending lectures on flight, putting theory into practice in a series of increasingly powerful machines, then finally going solo. Qualified pilots eventually progressed to a number of specialist schools, located particularly in south and south-west France, where they could train on particular aircraft types. Only then were they sent to the pool — the *Groupe de Divisions d'Entraînement* (GDE), situated in and around Le Plessis-Belleville (Oise), north of Paris — to await their posting to a front-line squadron.

Observers and bomb-aimers, recruited primarily among artillerymen to profit from their technical skills and knowledge, followed a different route. A specialist school was established at Le Plessis-Belleville, but qualified artillery observers were deemed to need little extra training. They were quickly posted to a squadron and could be operational very shortly afterwards.

(**Opposite**) Paris, 2013. Designed by Clément Ader (1841–1925), inveterate inventor and champion of air power, this steam-powered flying machine — *Avion III* — hangs proudly in the Musée des Arts et Métiers. Although *Avion* left the ground on its maiden flight in 1897, its pilot was never in full control of his craft. The steam engine also proved a dead end, but Ader left a permanent legacy in his coinage 'avion', which was adopted for official use in 1911 before being absorbed into the wider French language to replace the Anglophone 'aéroplane'.

Buc (Yvelines), 29 May 1911. Pictured (right to left) are General Pierre Roques (1856–1920), Captain Do Hûu Vi (1883–1916), Captain Félix Marie (1870–1938) and Captain Charles Marconnet. A notably energetic inspector of aviation from 1910 to 1912, Roques did much to prepare French aircraft and balloons for war. After transferring to a divisional command, he rose via XII Corps and First Army to become minister of war in 1916. Marie served as aviation commander of First Army in Alsace, and on the aviation staff. The Vietnamese Do served in Morocco, and with GB1. Seriously injured in a crash in 1915, he returned to his regiment, 1st Foreign Legion, but was killed on 9 July 1916, leading 7th Company in an attack at Belloy-en-Santerre (Somme).

(**Opposite, above**) Vincennes (Val-de-Marne), 9 June 1910. Lieutenant Albert Féquant (1886–1915) and Captain Charles Marconnet (1869–1914) are seated in their Farman, shortly after breaking the world distance record by covering 158km from Mourmelon (Marne) to Vincennes in 2.5 hours. This ground-breaking flight opened military eyes to the range, payload and potential of the new machines. The Farman made no real provision for a passenger, so Marconnet had to wedge himself in as best he could. Although a qualified pilot, he returned to 45th Infantry in 1914 and was killed in action at Carnoy (Somme) on 27 November. Féquant (VB102) remained in aviation, primarily in bomber units; he was killed returning from a long-distance raid on Saarbrücken on 6 September 1915.

(**Opposite, below**) Belfort (Territoire de Belfort). Admiring soldiers crowd around a Voisin biplane on the Champ de Mars. Captain Ferdinand Ferber (1862–1909) made the first flight from this key frontier fortress town (perhaps that depicted here) in July 1909. An artilleryman, aviation pioneer and correspondent of the Wright brothers, Ferber never designed a viable aircraft, but his example encouraged many others. He died in a flying accident at Beuvrequen (Pas-de-Calais) in September 1909. Belfort acquired a permanent landing ground in August 1912, home on the outbreak of war to two Blériot squadrons, BL3 and BL10.

General Édouard Hirschauer (1857–1943). An engineer and previously commander of the balloon service, Hirschauer was appointed inspector of aviation in April 1912. The lethargy of aircraft manufacturers frustrated his plans to expand the air service, and the rival artillery – coveting the aviation budget – accused him of collusion, forcing his resignation in August 1913. Fourteen months later Hirschauer returned as director of aviation, replacing General Félix Bernard (1857–1939) and doing much to put French manufacturers on a war footing. But again he was made a scapegoat – blamed for the vulnerability of French machines to the new Fokker Eindecker – and in September 1915 he was sacked. Hirschauer went on to serve with front-line formations, taking command of Second Army in December 1917. He ended his career as a politician, serving several terms as a senator for the Moselle.

(**Opposite, above**) Autumn manoeuvres, Sainte-Maure (Indre-et-Loire), September 1912. Piloted by Lieutenant Antonin Brocard (1885–1960), a Deperdussin TT of D6 lands at a temporary airfield. Brocard was appointed CO in March 1915 of MS/N3, then in 1916 of the celebrated *Groupement de Cachy*, later made permanent as GC12. In mid-1916, he chose a stork (*cigogne*) as the insignia of N3, and the bird was soon adopted in different variants by all the squadrons of GC12, which henceforth became known by that name. In 1917 he took a staff post as technical advisor to the recently appointed under-secretary of state, Jacques-Louis Dumesnil. The opposing forces in the 1912 manoeuvres, commanded by General Gallieni and General Marion, together deployed some 100,000 men and seventy-two aircraft. Each force comprised four squadrons, including the first five squadrons (Nos 1 to 5) of the newly independent air service, plus a number of scratch units.

(**Opposite, below**) Autumn manoeuvres, south-west France, September 1913. Ignoring a line of sentries, curious bystanders have managed to get close to the new machines, as soldiers and spectators combine to push a Blériot monoplane into the wind for take-off. During the manoeuvres, Red Force (including squadrons BL3, MF5 and HF19, plus the dirigible *Fleurus*) opposed Blue Force (including squadrons D6, V21 and BR17, plus the dirigible *Adjudant-Vincenot*).

A. Balussage, à Casablanca

(**Opposite, above**) Autumn manoeuvres, south-west France, September 1913. Preparing for the off, mechanics from HF19 reassemble a Henri Farman H.F.20, propped against cases of Benzol engine oil. Although aircraft had been included in these major exercises since 1910, the four-year cycle of manoeuvres and the lack of large-scale training facilities left many senior officers dangerously short of practical experience of working with the new technology.

(**Opposite, below**) Near Kasbah Tadla, Morocco, June 1913. Lieutenant Armand des Prez de la Morlais (1878–1963) has written off his Blériot monoplane while attempting to land. His defence was ready prepared: 'the temperature, very high inland, sets up violent thermals … making flying difficult, dangerous, at times impossible.' Morlais (BL18/VB102/EB13) was then CO of a small aviation detachment first sent to Morocco in 1912 to protect the Atlantic port of Mogador (now Essaouira) from rebellious tribesmen. He returned to France on the outbreak of war and later transferred to bombers.

(**Above**) Mourmelon (Marne), 1912. General Frédéric-Georges Herr (1855–1932) and Colonel Eugène Estienne (1860–1936) attend an aerial bombing competition. Estienne (right), the dynamic commander of the influential Vincennes research establishment, left aviation for good when war broke out and returned to the artillery. In 1915, he turned his inventive mind to tank development and is hailed as the father of French armour. Herr was just back from a trip to the Balkan War, where his observations of aircraft in action had convinced him of their spotting and reconnaissance value. In February 1916, he was sacked as commander of the fortress of Verdun, before resuming his career as an artillery advisor to General Pétain.

Lieutenant Charles de Tricornot de Rose (1876–1916). On 7 February 1911, de Rose – a dragoons officer – became the first pilot to earn his military wings, a couple of months after gaining his civilian license. He then joined Estienne at Vincennes, where he proved an innovative thinker, particularly in matters of air-to-air combat. Named CO of BL12 in August 1914, and aviation commander of Fifth Army that November, de Rose immediately began work to implement his theories. Equipping his squadron with the Morane-Saulnier Parasol, and then with the fast, manoeuvrable Nieuport, he effectively created France's first specialist fighter unit.

(**Opposite, above**) Roland Garros (1888–1918). Orginally from La Réunion, in the Indian Ocean, Garros (MS23/SPA26) bought a plane to teach himself to fly. He got off to an inauspicious start: 'After scarcely 30 metres a huge biplane came in to land ... I couldn't get away and he landed right on top of me, cutting my machine in half and reducing it to matchwood.' Nevertheless, Garros earned his civilian license in 1910 and within months was making his name as a pilot: winning air races, setting altitude records and in 1913 becoming the first man to cross the Mediterranean. Before the war he worked with de Rose on methods of arming aircraft, continuing his researches over the winter of 1914–15 while serving with MS23.

(**Opposite, below**) Dr Émile Reymond (1865–1914). Reymond, pre-war chair of the senate aviation committee, had learned to fly for sport. He joined BL9 as a volunteer in August 1914, armed himself with a carbine and a revolver, and soon spotted an Aviatik over the Meurthe valley: 'I ... aimed for the pilot. The plane dived off ... To our right, another German was closing fast, nearer this time, around the same height. Switching [the carbine] to my left shoulder, I targeted the hub of the propeller. I missed ... I took out my revolver and aimed carefully ... squeezing off all six rounds from around 80 metres. The plane dived, banking sharply.' Reymond had missed his target again, and both enemy machines escaped. On 21 October 1914, he and his pilot were killed by ground fire after their plane was forced down between the lines.

92

Lieutenant Marcel Brindejonc des Moulinais (1892–1916). Seen here with his Dorand DO.1, Brindejonc des Moulinais (DO22/N23) had earned his wings in March 1911, after just two months' training. He soon achieved fame as a long-distance flyer, winning the Coupe Pommery in 1913 by covering 1,382km from Paris to Warsaw at an average speed of 170km/h. By mid-August 1914, 'overjoyed to be at war' after the boredom of barracks life, he was posted to DO22, serving with Fourth Army in the Ardennes. Yet his initial enthusiasm soon began to fade. 'Dead in spirit,' he was admitted to hospital in June 1915. 'Eventually I decided that I'm just dog-tired. It's this lousy war.' Transferring to N23, he was killed over Verdun in 1916. Contemporary reports blamed component failure, but he may well have fallen victim to friendly fire.

(**Opposite, above**) A Breguet U.2 of BR17 takes to the skies, 1914. On the outbreak of war, BR17 was attached to First Army in Alsace. Within a fortnight, however, the army commander, General Auguste Dubail (1851–1934), was reporting the U.2 'unfit for active service'; his crews, he claimed, viewed it with 'great apprehension'. BR17 was disbanded in November 1914, and its Breguets consigned to the scrapheap. Equipped with the Voisin 3 bomber, the squadron was subsequently reformed as VB3 (later VB103).

(**Opposite, below**) Beaumetz-lès-Loges (Pas-de-Calais), 1915. Although aircraft were painted with prominent national markings from the first days of the war, they always remained vulnerable to the troops on the ground, who tended to blaze away at friend as well as foe. 'Our men are still firing up at us whenever we fly overhead,' grumbled Lieutenant Alfred Zapelli (D6), on 4 September 1914. Enough was enough, he decided. 'I've had my roundels repainted four times larger,' he reported the following day. '[Now they're] 2 metres wide.'

Sergeant Joseph Frantz (1890–1979) and Corporal Louis Quenault (1892–1958). Frantz (left, pilot) and Quenault (right, observer), both of V24, have just achieved the first confirmed victory in air-to-air combat, over Jonchery-sur-Vesle (Marne), on 5 October 1914. Here, they pose beside the rudder of their Voisin 3. A pre-war test pilot, Frantz made his name by breaking several endurance records. Although later credited with a second victory, he soon returned to testing duties with Farman. Quenault abandoned front-line flying in 1915 and was posted as a mechanic to Villacoublay (Yvelines).

(**Opposite, above**) Avord (Cher). An officer and NCO pilots are pictured at this military flying school established in October 1912. The earliest military pilots had trained at schools opened by the aircraft manufacturers. By 1910, however, the civilian license was deemed insufficiently taxing and a special military qualification was introduced, with dedicated schools at Pau (Pyrénées-Atlantiques) and Avord. Under Captain Georges Bellenger (1878–1977), a key member of Estienne's pre-war Vincennes research team and later aviation commander of Sixth Army, the Avord school specialized in training pilots for the Blériot squadrons: BL3, BL9, BL10 and Bellenger's own BL18. When the Blériots were declared obsolete in late 1914, it became the main training centre for pilots destined for Caudron squadrons.

(**Opposite, below**) Buc (Yvelines). A mixed line-up of Blériot and REP monoplanes await their pupils at this school established by manufacturer Louis Blériot in 1912, and militarized in 1915. Nicknamed 'Château Blériot', the large building to the rear served as an accommodation block for students and instructors alike. The airfield was returned to private use in 1948 (although an army aviation detachment continued to be based there) and closed in the 1960s. It has since been built over.

(**Above**) Buc (Yvelines), 1916. An instructor lectures his student in an REP – a little finger-wagging serves to emphasize the point. Students began their practical instruction in these 'penguins' – an airframe whose wingspan was cut down to prevent take-off – then progressed through a series of increasingly more powerful machines until judged capable of flying solo. Charles Biddrich (N73) found the penguins rather hard to handle: 'At first you go sideways and twist around in each direction except the one in which you wish to go. After you catch on … however, you go tripping along … at some 30 or 40 miles an hour.'

(**Opposite**) Étampes (Essonne), November 1915. The Farman school, pictured here, was opened by Henry Farman in March 1910 at Mondésir, south-west of Étampes. Three months later, Louis Blériot opened a rival school on the opposite side of the road. Both schools were militarized in 1915: the Farman school trained French pilots in conjunction with the former Deperdussin school at nearby Guinette, while the Blériot school was turned over to the Belgians. The Farman field at Mondésir remains in use today; the Deperdussin field closed after the First World War and the Blériot field closed after the Second World War.

(**Opposite, above**) Étampes (Essonne), 27 February 1917. Colonel Adolphe Girod (1872–1933), inspector of schools, casts a beady eye over a line-up of trainee pilots. A Radical parliamentary deputy for the Doubs from 1906 to 1928, Girod was recalled in 1914, serving as commander of GB1 from September 1914, and aviation commander of the CRP from October 1914. Appointed director of schools in September 1915, he quickly reorganized and reinvigorated this vital aspect of the aviation service.

(**Opposite, below**) Étampes (Essonne), 16 September 1915. Despite its transfer to Belgian control, the former Blériot school retained some French personnel as instructors. Here, a group including chief pilot Sergeant Pierre Gouguenheim (in horizon blue, centre) pose before an ill-used Maurice Farman M.F.11 – a machine reportedly retired from front-line service with 300 patches on its fabric. A pre-war test pilot for Farman, Gouguenheim (1892–1962) had seen front-line service with DO/MF22 before being posted to the school in 1915.

(**Above**) Étampes (Essonne), 1916. An instructor takes charge in a Farman M.F.11. The M.F.11 was the standard French cooperation type from early 1915 until 1917, but it also served as a light bomber, and even as a fighter. Some machines were modified (as here) to a dual-control system. Two grips were fitted to the single control column, forcing the instructor to reach awkwardly around his pupil. On 26 April 1915, Étampes was the scene of Philippe Connen's first flight, in an M.F.12: 'I've flown! I've flown,' reported Connen (1895–1975). 'I didn't particularly enjoy it … "Strap yourself in tight," shouted [my instructor, Lepeintre]. But I didn't know how, so I wasn't happy. "Mind your helmet!" But I was constantly worried that the propeller wash would snatch it off.'

(**Above**) Étampes (Essonne), 27 February 1917. A Farman M.F.7 circles at a height of 300m above the flying school. Although by then obsolete in terms of front-line service, the Farman remained a stable, robust craft ideal for pilot training. 'The lap consisted of a circuit of a little wood lying east of the hangars,' continued Connen. 'Half an hour later, Lepeintre took me up in the 50hp M.F.1. This time I took the controls. Really, though, I wasn't as happy as I expected. I need more practice.'

(**Opposite, above**) Buc (Yvelines), 14 June 1911. No plane could withstand a head-on collision with a hangar, even a type as robust as a Farman. Flying was an inherently dangerous activity: wartime accidents killed some 15 per cent of all student pilots, and almost 2,900 men in the service as a whole, fully 60 per cent of all aviation casualties. Jacques Gobilliard (1893–1965) served with F/AR/SAL32. 'Worst are the Breguets which catch fire in the air … and the Nieuport two-seaters that break in half, also in flight … Scarcely more inviting are the Farmans with their rear-mounted engine and protruding fuselage, with the observer seated in front of the pilot … a nose-over and the poor observer is crushed in the nose of the plane. A bad accident and the pilot … will be hit by the engine … he's still better off than his observer though, and ten times less likely to cop it.'

(**Opposite, below**) Ground-crew training. Trainees receive electrical instruction. Initial ground-crew training took place at one of the three aviation service depots: Saint-Cyr-l'École (Yvelines), Dijon-Longvic (Côte d'Or) or Lyon-Bron (Rhône). Saint-Cyr was one of France's earliest military airfields, home of a pre-war depot as well as the Zodiac dirigible factory. Longvic was a pre-war operational base, which became a supply and training depot in August 1914 after its four squadrons were dispersed among the armies; a pilot training school opened there in 1916. Bron was a fort completed in 1877, situated on the east bank of the Rhône.

Ground-crew training. An NCO (left) describes the workings of an engine to his pupils. Training offered a mixture of theory and practice. Pupils studied geometry, mechanics and aerodynamics; they also learned about engines in general; the specific Renault, Clerget, Hispano-Suiza and Salmson types; and fabric and rigging. Successful candidates then progressed to specialist training, often at a manufacturer's facility.

Ground-crew training, Grivesnes (Somme), September 1916. A mixed group of artillerymen and engineers study the theory of wireless telegraphy. In its infancy before the war, the use of wireless telegraphy to transmit and receive from aircraft grew rapidly in importance, particularly for artillery spotting. 'Our electrician NCOs sometimes took us to a hut, gathered us around a mysterious little box, and tried to drill us in the basics of this fledgling technology, wireless telegraphy,' recalled Sapper Jean Poncin (5th Engineers). 'Without necessarily grasping it all, we found it enormously interesting. And it made us feel superior to the two thousand-odd poor devils in the other ground-to-ground companies, whose only tasks were climbing poles and stringing wire. We felt like the elite of some primitive society.'

Chapter Two

Nailed to the sky

The competing missions initially envisaged for military aviation – reconnaissance and artillery spotting – shared the common purpose of supporting the troops on the ground, and the cooperation squadrons that performed these roles formed a key component of the air service throughout the conflict, developing rapidly under the pressure of war in terms of aircraft, equipment, tactics, communication and organization.

Contrary to pre-war expectations, a renascent balloon service also played its part. Expecting a short, mobile encounter, French commanders had disbanded the balloon field companies shortly before the outbreak of war, mothballing the static balloons and halting all further production: only the four fortress companies remained operational. The rapid onset of trench warfare, however, forced a change of heart. The balloon service was reinstated and expanded, initially deploying the existing 1880-pattern Type E balloon. Another pre-war design – the man-bearing kite – also had its adherents, but like the Type E it was unstable in windy conditions, as was the new Type H balloon – a copy of the sausage-shaped German *drachen* – introduced in 1915. Only in 1916 did the French finally overcome these failings with the arrival of Albert Caquot's innovative Type M, which offered a stable platform in all but the most extreme conditions, as well as a powerful, petrol-driven winch.

Static balloons also offered a significant advantage denied to aircraft – a telephone line providing a swift and effective two-way voice link with the ground. Morse sets, powered by a wind-driven generator mounted on the nose or upper wing of a plane, were beginning to appear on the scene. They were trialled on the Aisne front in November 1914, used by V24 to control the fall of shot for I Corps artillery, then gradually introduced into the service. Otherwise communication methods remained crude and inflexible: pilots manoeuvred in the air or dropped messages to the troops below, who in turn employed strips of white cloth arranged on the ground according to a predetermined code.

In the field of photo-reconnaissance, however, aircraft quickly proved their worth. The earliest experiments were conducted on private initiative in September 1914, but the French commander-in-chief General Joseph Joffre quickly grasped their importance both for reconnaissance and for updating maps. In the short term, the potential of aerial photography was limited by the technology available: glass plate negatives, which were heavy and awkward to handle in the air; and short lenses, which demanded vertical shots taken directly above the subject. But plates were soon replaced by film, greatly increasing the return from each mission – over 5,000 photographs were distributed to front-line infantry and artillery formations prior to the Champagne offensive in September 1915, for example. Lenses also improved significantly in length and quality, enabling crews to fly higher, to avoid anti-aircraft fire, and to take oblique shots of more distant enemy positions without the need to overfly and advertise their interest. By 1916, photo-reconnaissance machines could penetrate up to 25km into German-held territory. Meanwhile, from 1915 interpretation was handled by dedicated sections attached to each army and army corps, liaising with intelligence and operations staffs, and transmitting new information to mapping sections. With speed vital, many squadrons also included a mobile developing unit.

All these missions – whether reconnaissance, spotting or photo-reconnaissance – demanded a stable platform with good endurance, the chief virtues of the Farmans and Caudrons that formed the mainstay of the early cooperation squadrons. Sadly, these strengths were not matched by similar defensive qualities, and from the summer of 1915 both types proved easy prey for the new Fokker Eindecker, which also had the better of the Nieuport 10 – a fast two-seater reconnaissance aircraft, armed with a machine gun fired by the observer, but powered by a rotary engine that made it unsuitable for all but the most experienced pilots.

The German onslaught on Verdun, launched on 21 February 1916, put enormous pressure on the cooperation squadrons – spotter and reconnaissance machines alike. With the collapse of the intelligence network in occupied France and Belgium, and with the reconnaissance crews grounded by weeks of bad weather, the French were taken almost completely by surprise. Swamping their opponents with their initial attacks, the Germans quickly established total air superiority. Then they changed tactics, using two-seater barrier patrols to block access to their lines, with a supporting force of Fokker and Pfalz monoplanes ready to intercept any successful intruder. Meanwhile the enemy guns, firing in pairs, targeted the remaining balloons – one aiming at the envelope, the other at the winch.

By 25 February, another thirty-two squadrons had been despatched to Verdun – twenty-six reconnaissance units, five for artillery spotting and one for photo-reconnaissance – and the energetic General Philippe Pétain (1856–1951) had arrived to command all ground and air troops throughout the sector. Pétain set to work at once, ordering his planes to reconnoitre enemy movements by road and rail, identify any movements of enemy batteries, photograph new units and battery positions, establish a barrier and attack any intruder penetrating French lines. He also realized that his squadrons had a role to play in improving front-line morale: 'If bad weather halts reconnaissance missions, the planes can still wheel round and overfly the troops, even at low altitudes.'

Innovatively, Pétain divided his front into several 'army corps sectors', each with its own aerial component – one army corps squadron, ten to fifteen machines strong, one or two smaller heavy artillery flights to spot for his big guns, two or three balloon companies and one or two divisional squadrons – about fifty planes in all. The new system ensured greater continuity of command, improved internal communications and facilitated local intelligence gathering, in general functioning so well that it was retained for the rest of the war.

Throughout 1916 and 1917, the conflict continued to accelerate the development of single-seater fighters – like the German Albatros or the French Nieuports and SPADs – to protect friendly machines and to interdict the enemy. At the same time, the French were also seeking a cooperation aircraft capable of looking after itself. A handful of designs eventually saw service, including the A.R. and the giant, multi-engine Letord, but without success: the A.R. was obsolete on its arrival at the front, while so large was the Letord that no squadron could be equipped solely with that type – airfields were simply not big enough to cope. Only in early 1918, with the introduction of the Breguet 14 and Salmson 2A.2, did the situation finally begin to improve.

(**Opposite**) Merval (Aisne), August 1915. The French entered the war equipped only with these 1880-pattern, spherical Type E balloons. Despite a relatively high operational ceiling of 800m, they were unstable in any wind over 30km/h and controlled by a horse-drawn steam winch. About to be scrapped in August 1914, the balloon field companies were hurriedly reinstated, their existing Type E balloons brought out of storage and new orders placed.

(**Above**) Bray (Pas-de-Calais), February 1916. A train of man-bearing kites takes to the sky. These kites were flimsy affairs, consisting of a small one-man basket suspended beneath a chain of fabric-covered frames. They served in small numbers with some balloon companies, and also with the navy. Although a useful platform in fine weather, they were more fragile than balloons, had a lower operating ceiling, and could fly only in wind speeds ranging from 36km/h to 72km/h.

(**Opposite, above**) Bray (Pas-de-Calais), February 1916. Swathed in fur as protection from the cold, an observer leaves the ground beneath a train of man-bearing kites. Marc Brillaud de Laujardière 'went up to 600m in one of these contraptions on 9 May 1915 during the Artois offensive, but the wind was so gusty I spent all my time adjusting the cables. Observation was almost impossible as well as a complete waste of time.' The observer was linked to the ground by telephone, but early in the war messages were carried from that point by runner.

(**Opposite, below**) Merval (Aisne), August 1915. A balloon is inflated with hydrogen. Each tube contained 150m^3 of gas, and 130 to 140 tubes were needed in all – an operation that could take up to three hours. The eventual introduction of mobile gas tankers slashed the time required to just thirty minutes.

(**Opposite, above**) Châlons-le-Vergeur (Marne), January 1916. A Type H balloon is readied for its ascent. Once inflated, the balloon was 'walked' to its ascension point by the men of the company, who then held it in place while the observer climbed into the basket – an event that here has attracted quite a crowd. 'So formless at ground level, the "sausage" soars into the wide blue yonder and takes shape. Attached to its steel cable, it expands and disappears from view.'

(**Opposite, below**) Chenay (Marne), June 1917. Every balloon company included a single-winch vehicle, here an example based on a Latil T9 chassis. Captain Jacques Saconney (1874–1935), commander of the revamped balloon service, introduced two models of petrol-driven winch, mounting the engine from a Panhard lorry on a chassis, first a Delahaye, then a Latil: 45th–54th Companies, which were mixed balloon/kite units, used the Saconney-Delahaye winch; 55th–94th Companies used the Latil. The slow, horse-drawn 1878-pattern steam-powered winch, used at the start of the war, remained in service with the pre-war companies, 1st–24th.

(**Above**) La Neuville-au-Pont (Marne), May 1916. A new Type M balloon of 60th Balloon Company (IV Corps), carrying Sergeant Bonnemaison, enjoys a clear view over the Aisne and the Bionne valleys, looking north-west towards the Main de Massiges. 'The visibility was very good, bright sunshine, not a cloud in the sky, so I could see over 50km,' reported another observer. 'The basket was perfectly stable. It didn't move an inch. I felt like I'd been nailed to the sky. It was marvellous.'

(**Above**) Ferme de Vadenay (Marne), May 1917. Binoculars in hand, a trainee observer in a static balloon consults his map and talks to his ground station. His parachute hangs over the left of the basket in a canvas bag. Situated on the edge of the massive camp at Châlons-sur Marne (now Châlons-en-Champagne), the Ferme de Vadenay school was established for observers on 1 May 1916. It was extended the following year to include all balloon specialists – mechanics, riggers, telephonists and machine-gunners. By 1918, it also housed sheds containing massive painted panoramas, allowing instruction to continue in bad weather.

(**Opposite**) Chalais-Meudon (Hauts-de-Seine), June 1917. A soldier resignedly tests a parachute harness. Static-line parachutes were first provided in 1916 for use if enemy action set fire to the balloon, but observers initially viewed them with some scepticism. Assisted by Seaman Constant Duclos, Lieutenant Georges Juchmès of the balloon service depot at Chalais-Meudon was required to perform as many as twenty-eight demonstration jumps to convince his peers. By the end of the war, it was possible to detach the whole basket and descend it by parachute.

(**Above**) Haudainville (Meuse), May 1916. The telephonists of 52nd Balloon Company are pictured inside their exchange. The company was then positioned between the village and the fort of the same name, part of the outer ring of Verdun's right-bank defences. Despite the rainy, blustery weather, the balloons ascended almost daily to report on enemy movements, spending 185 hours aloft that month. A line ran from the basket, down the mooring cable and to the exchange; lines proceeded from here to individual artillery batteries and to headquarters, allowing observer and gunner to converse. Wireless was introduced in 1916, but to little effect; wireless transmissions were vulnerable to enemy interception and so needed coding, slowing down the whole process.

(**Opposite, above**) Eulmont (Meurthe-et-Moselle), May 1917. Men in the company office of 71st Balloon Company consult incoming reports. Behind them, on the wall, are their sector map and panorama. The company was situated in what was then a quiet sector. It performed some artillery spotting for 81st Division artillery, but poor weather conditions often restricted the amount of observation work possible.

(**Opposite, below**) A pilot and observer struggle into their flying gear before taking off in their Farman. Even in high summer, air temperatures at altitude were freezing. Many aircrew needed help from their mechanic to prepare, as layer followed upon layer in the effort to keep warm. 'We lumbered about like deep-sea divers,' grumbled one pilot.

(**Opposite, above**) Baslieux-lès-Fismes (Marne), summer 1915. A Caudron G.3 is started up. The plane belongs to C6, then employed on spotting missions for XVIII Corps. The G.3 was a stalwart of the cooperation squadrons during 1915, prized for its stability and field of vision. Although produced in quantity in France, Italy and the UK, the type was relatively slow and unarmed and quickly became obsolete. Withdrawn from front-line service in 1916, it continued in use as a trainer.

(**Opposite, below**) Hermaville (Pas-de-Calais), May 1915. Maurice Farman M.F.11, MF320, prepares to take off on reconnaissance during the battle of Artois. The plane belongs to MF35, then working for XX Corps, part of Tenth Army. The pilot and observer make one last check of their map before ordering the mechanic to swing the propeller. Visible in the background are the squadron's Bessonneau hangars.

(**Above**) Baconnes (Marne), April 1917. Artillery batteries communicated with aircraft by arranging cloth panels according to a pre-set code. Here, they show that a railway artillery battery, just visible in front of the distant wood, is ready to fire. 'To indicate the guns were firing to the right, you turned right; the gunners had cloth sheets. It was all pretty hit-and-miss,' remembered pilot Paul Gambier (C28/106/64). But the arrival of wireless telegraphy made a huge difference: 'We could talk in code between the ground and the air … it was clear as the nose on your face.'

Jules Védrines (1881–1919). Among the most prominent of pre-war pilots, Védrines (DO22/MS/N3) triumphed in the 1911 Paris–Madrid race and undertook long-range flights to Prague and Cairo. During the conflict, he specialized in dropping agents behind enemy lines. His first aircraft was a heavily armoured Blériot 36bis, nicknamed *La Vache* (The Cow). A cow – displayed here on his Nieuport 11 – remained his personal badge.

(**Opposite, above**) Art-sur-Meurthe (Meurthe-et-Moselle), 1917. This exercise in ground-to-air signalling uses Ruggieri smoke-pots, devices lit by the advancing infantry to keep aircraft flying contact patrols abreast of progress on the ground. This worked well in good conditions, but if gas, smoke, explosions and mud reduced visibility, extra measures were required. The Ruggieri fireworks company, first established in Paris in 1739, is still in operation today. The firm also manufactured illuminating shells, flares and rockets for the army.

(**Opposite, below**) Marc Pourpe (1887–1914). A barnstorming pilot in Indochina and the Middle East, Pourpe came to fame by flying from Cairo to Khartoum in January 1914, when his mechanic was the young American Raoul Lufbery (VB106/N124). Pourpe joined MS23 on the outbreak of war, flying reconnaissance missions. Wounded in September, he was killed on 2 December, alongside his observer Lieutenant Eugène Vauglin (1884–1914), crashing in bad weather while attempting to land at Villers-Bretonneux (Somme).

Lieutenant Charles Dumas (1891–1916). Seen here with his observer in their Caudron, Dumas (C11/N57) had transferred to aviation from 57th Artillery, initially as an observer, before gaining his wings in January 1916. He was posted to N57, then sent on attachment to C4, flying missions over Verdun from the squadron's base at Ancemont (Meuse). He was shot down and killed on patrol over Hennemont (Meuse) on 25 August 1916; his body was recovered and buried by the German authorities.

Above Le Hamel (Somme), 1916. An observer takes a snap of his pilot in their Caudron G.4. Two squadrons – C17 and C53 – operated from this airfield. The G.4 was developed from the obsolescent Caudron G.3. Rather than a single engine mounted on the nose, it had two engines mounted between the wings – an arrangement allowing more room for the observer and for fitting defensive armament (the drum of a rear-facing Lewis machine gun is clearly visible here). With its extra power, the G.4 could also carry a bomb load, and the type was primarily used in this capacity. Its persistent lack of speed, however, left it vulnerable to enemy fighters.

Vaux-sur-Somme (Somme), April 1916. Lieutenant Pierre Perrin de Brichambaut (1889–1967) is pictured in his ravaged Farman. On an artillery spotting mission over Tilloy (Pas-de-Calais) in 1915, Perrin de Brichambaut (MF8/99) had turned his aircraft into a strong westerly wind, rendering it almost stationary in the air. Ideal for spotting the fall of shot, this manoeuvre also made him a perfect target and his machine was soon peppered with shrapnel. One near-miss too many convinced him that it was time to depart. He made it back to the airfield, but later confessed that 'after climbing down from the plane that day, I couldn't hang on to my much-abused breakfast any longer'.

(**Opposite, above**) Nieuwpoort (West-Vlaanderen), October 1916. The pilot of this Farman F.40 of MF36, *Ça Va Gazer* (*Speed Merchant*), lost control at 3,200m but managed to level out and land safely at an airfield just inside Allied lines. His lucky mascot is visible on the nose of the plane. The machine nosed over on landing, leaving the dent in the nacelle. The F.40 was developed as an 'improved' version of the F.11. It proved no better than its predecessor, but was still introduced into service in late 1915. MF36 was re-equipped with Sopwiths in July 1917.

(**Opposite, below**) General Victor Boëlle (1850–1942). Boëlle, the commander of IV Corps, speaks to a pilot from MF22. Before the introduction of wireless telegraphy, crews were required to land and report in person to a general. Based at Châlons-sur-Marne (Marne), MF22 had converted to Farmans from the unloved Dorand in November 1914. In the background is MF153, the favourite machine of the squadron CO, Lieutenant René Drouot (1883–?), who spent much of the winter of 1914–15 testing new shell-spotting techniques for the artillery.

(**Above**) Ferme de Saint-Amand, Saconin-Breuil (Aisne), November 1917. The photographic officer of SPA62 presents the three main cameras used by reconnaissance squadrons. The hand-held camera of 25cm focal length served to capture general views of the enemy lines. For a more detailed image of a particular trench, a camera of 50cm focal length (right) was used. The largest camera (left), 1.2m in focal length, was capable of isolating individual positions.

(**Above**) Brocourt-en-Argonne (Meuse), May 1916. A Maurice Farman MF11 prepares to leave the airfield. The plane belongs to the newly redesignated F33, part of IX Corps, then flying photographic reconnaissance missions over the Verdun sector. The observer is Lieutenant Nissim de Camondo (1892–1917), recently transferred from 21st Dragoons, and later a pilot in the same squadron. He and his observer Sous-lieutenant Louis des Essarts would be shot down and killed over Leintrey (Meurthe-et-Moselle) on 5 September 1917. The Musée Nissim de Camondo in Paris was later named in his honour by his banker father, Moïse.

(**Opposite, above**) Combles (Somme), 13 October 1916. The village of Combles had fallen in late September to an Anglo-French attack, before serving as a starting point on 6 October for a French assault on positions in and around Sailly-Saillisel, just visible in the distance. After heavy, see-saw fighting over the next six weeks, French troops managed to capture Sailly, only to lose many of their gains to German counter-attacks.

(**Opposite, below**) Craonne (Aisne), 4 June 1917. The pale smear in the middle ground is all that remains of the village of Craonne after the ill-fated Chemin des Dames offensive, launched in April by General Robert Nivelle (1856–1924), newly appointed in place of General Joffre as French commander-in-chief; the hill behind is the Plateau de Californie. Both village and hill became bywords for the catastrophic assault and the heavy casualties incurred.

COMBLES.-

(**Opposite, above**) Ferme de Saint-Amand, near Saconin-Breuil (Aisne), November 1917. Lieutenant Charles Borzecki (1881–1959), of SPA62, gets ready for take-off while his camera is loaded aboard a new SPAD 11. The SPAD 11 was a scaled-up version of the SPAD 7 fighter. Although tail-heavy and lacking manoeuvrability, it was still superior to its A.R. and Sopwith predecessors. SPA62 used a cockerel badge throughout the war; this particular design, introduced in 1917, was the work of one of its observers, Sergeant Georges Boutin (1879–?), an architect in civilian life.

(**Opposite, below**) Saconin-Breuil (Aisne), November 1917. A Berliet ICB mobile photographic laboratory attached to SPA62. In times of great urgency, the lab could develop and print twenty individual images in twenty-four minutes; the prints were good enough to convey immediate information, but short-cuts in fixing meant they would not last long. For photographs of record, a more considered approach allowed the lab to turn out ten prints apiece of fifty different images in six hours.

(**Above**) Rexpoëde (Nord), August 1917. The men of First Army's cartographic section update their maps with new intelligence gleaned by the reconnaissance crews. Even if prevented from taking photographs by bad weather or enemy action, the observer was still expected to gather information. In addition to the pre-war 1:80,000 series, maps were produced in three other main scales – 1:20,000 for the artillery, 1:10,000 for the infantry, and highly detailed 1:5,000 sheets for individual operations. Maps showing geology and hydrology were also developed for some areas of the front.

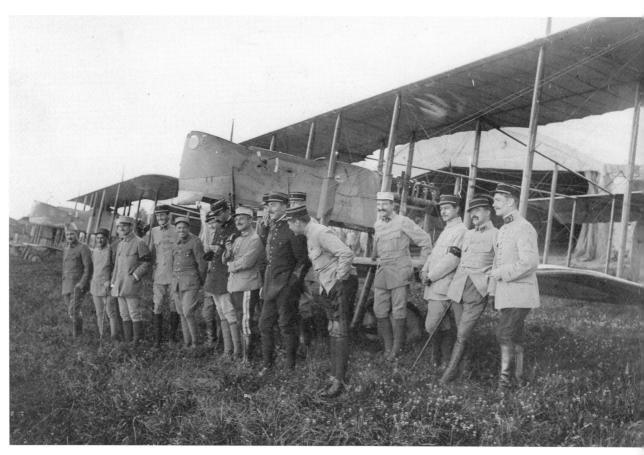

(**Opposite, above**) Saint-Clément (Meurthe-et-Moselle), 21 August 1916. In the dark uniform (seventh from right), Captain Maurice Marquer (1876–?), CO of MF41, lines up with his pilots and observers. Within a month, the squadron would transfer to the Somme front as part of XXXII Corps. In December 1916, MF41 replaced its Farman M.F.40 with the new Dorand A.R.1.

(**Opposite, below**) Hourges (Marne), June 1917. Lieutenant Philippe de Forceville (pilot, centre) is pictured with his brand-new Dorand AR1. His squadron F33 has just converted to the new type, renumbering as AR33. The squadron badge, a boarding axe (*hache d'abordage*), was adopted in late 1916 as a pun on the name of then squadron CO Alfred Bordage. Although an improvement on its Farman predecessors, the A.R. had spent so long in development that it was almost obsolete by the time it reached front-line units. AR33 had just received its new machines, but within six months would exchange them for Salmsons.

(**Above**) Treslon (Marne), 23 May 1917. Aircrew of Heavy Artillery Flight 228 pose in front of a new Letord L.1. The Letords were distributed among some twenty-five different units, just one or two apiece to avoid impossible overcrowding on the airfields. Primarily equipped with Caudrons, Heavy Artillery Flight 228 specialized in artillery work, spotting for 84th Heavy Artillery Regiment in Champagne. In 1917 it expanded to a squadron, converting in January 1918 to SPAD two-seaters, then in July to Breguets.

(**Above**) Le Plessis-Belleville (Oise), June 1918. Personnel of AR14 pose in the squadron office. The squadron was then completing its conversion from the obsolete A.R.1 to the new Salmson 2A.2, in the process changing its designation to SAL14. Attached to 46th Alpine Infantry Division, AR14 had spent time on the Italian front. It had recently taken part in the third battle of Flanders (the German 'Georgette' offensive, 9–29 April 1918) and would go on to see action in the fourth battle of Champagne (the 'Friedensturm' offensive, 15–18 July 1918), the final enemy offensive in the west.

(**Opposite, above**) Baslieux-lès-Fismes (Marne), 1915. The men of C6 are still housed in tents, rather than huts. The village, behind the trees in the background, was too small to accommodate them. The squadron spent a year here, from May 1915 to May 1916, supporting the operations of XVIII Corps north of Reims. In 1917, Corporal Charles Biddle was stationed close to Bergues (Nord): 'My tent is in a field next to some farm buildings, and the pasture is full of horses, cows and three or four big fat sows. The latter are very inquisitive … we came in one day to find them all asleep in our tent.'

(**Opposite, below**) Souilly (Meuse), September 1917. The aircraft of N23 and R210 are pictured outside their uncamouflaged hangars. The crews are housed in the huts lined up opposite the hangars in the foreground. At the top of the image is the entrance to an underground munitions magazine. Work on the airfield at Souilly began in early 1916, using a site close to roads, but safe from enemy artillery, and incidentally close to Second Army headquarters. Construction advanced rapidly after the German assault on Verdun, and the airfield was soon in active service. After the war it was returned to agricultural use.

(**Opposite, above**) Vadelaincourt (Meuse), May 1916. German prisoners-of-war are employed to maintain the landing ground at this key airfield, south-west of Verdun. Few French airfields used hard-standing or runways in the modern sense; consequently, heavy rain could restrict operations by making it difficult for aircraft to take off and land. Potholes and molehills were further hazards for aircrew: 'the smallest furrow or clod of earth can produce a nose-over or break the propeller,' claimed the journalist 'Pol'. 'In winter a frozen molehill can scythe off the undercarriage.'

(**Above**) Faverolles-et-Coëmy (Marne), March 1917. A Bessonneau hangar is under construction. Developed and produced by the textile firm of the same name, based in Angers (Maine-et-Loire), the Bessonneau's easily transportable, prefabricated modular design allowed it to be built with six, nine or twelve bays as required. Most common was the six-bay variant, with interior dimensions 20m^2. Each squadron had several hangars – normally six or seven – their number and size determined by the number and size of the planes.

(**Opposite, below**) Ferme de la Cense (Marne), 12 April 1917. A Bessonneau hangar has collapsed in high winds at this airfield near Fismes, with unhappy consequences for a Caudron of C6. The bad weather of March and April played havoc with reconnaissance and spotting missions before and during Nivelle's catastrophic Chemin des Dames offensive.

(**Above**) Lunéville (Meurthe-et-Moselle), 30 August 1915. Captain Alphonse Vanduick (1880–1916), CO of MF45, is pictured in his office tent. Originally an infantryman, Vanduick (left) was MF45's first CO, serving from its birth in April 1915 until November 1915. He transferred to the staff in Paris, where he was killed in an accident in July 1916.

(**Opposite, above**) Lunéville (Meurthe-et-Moselle), 2 September 1915. Captain Vanduick (seated, centre) and his officers are busy in the squadron office, writing reports or updating maps. In the background hangs their flying gear: leather flying helmets and heavy leather or fur coats. Seated (right) at the captain's table is a pupil observer, seconded from 2nd Artillery Regiment as part of his training – either Sous-lieutenant Jean Rey or Sous-lieutenant Georges Oppermann, both then serving with the squadron.

(**Opposite, below**) Lunéville (Meurthe-et-Moselle), September 1915. The supplies officer of MF45 works on his ledgers. At his side are cases of Automobiline ('the petrol you can trust') and Motricine ('the queen of petrols'), with spare parts neatly arrayed on the shelves behind him. Engines still used conventional petrol: commercially viable aviation spirit had yet to be invented. Rotary engines consumed between 25 and 35 litres of petrol and 6 litres of oil per hour; in-line engines, like the Hispano-Suiza, between 40 and 70 litres of petrol, depending on engine capacity.

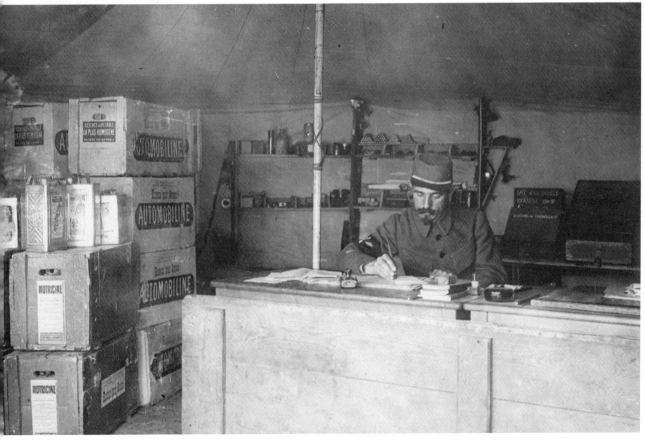

(**Opposite, above**) Lunéville (Meurthe-et-Moselle), September 1915. The motor transport of an unknown squadron is lined up neatly here: five trailers for spare wings and fuselages, seven light Renault CT lorries (known throughout the aviation service as *breaks*), and a couple of Berliet or Chenard et Walker runabouts.

(**Opposite, below**) Villers-lès-Nancy (Meurthe-et-Moselle), 1917. Three machine guns – two Hotchkiss and one Lewis – are mounted on stands in the armourer's workshop of C9. Spare drums of ammunition for the Lewis gun are stored on the wall behind. Based at this airfield, C9 performed long-range reconnaissance missions for XXXIX Corps over what was then a relatively quiet sector of the front.

(**Above**) Villers-lès-Nancy (Meurthe-et-Moselle), 1917. A mechanic is hard at work in C9's workshop, housed in a hangar. There were two dedicated mechanics for each aircraft, led by Quartermaster Sergeant Eugène Chalon and four corporals. C9 was nominally equipped with the Caudron G.6, but it also included on its strength several Sopwith 1½-Strutters (redesignated by the French as the Sopwith 1A.2). As SOP9, it was re-equipped entirely with that type during the summer of 1917. XXXIX Corps moved north to the Aisne in August 1917, taking part in the Malmaison offensive in late October. The squadron exchanged its Sopwiths for Breguets in May 1918.

Chapter Three

Giving them something to think about

Conceived initially as a means of providing battlefield assistance to the army, aircraft were very quickly used to strike directly at the enemy. The first French raid took place on 14 August 1914, when Lieutenant Antoine Cesari and Corporal Roger Prudhommeaux (MF16) decided to drop a load of modified 155mm artillery shells on the Zeppelin hangars at Metz-Frescaty. The seven French dirigible balloons were also soon in action, the *Adjudant-Vincenot* and the *Fleurus* 1 venturing as far as Sarrebourg and Trier. However, the dirigibles were highly vulnerable to ground fire – from friend and foe alike – and when the *Dupuy-de-Lôme* was downed by the defenders of Reims on the night of 23–24 August, the entire fleet was grounded. Missions resumed in April 1915, targeting railway lines and other infrastructure objectives. Although confined to night operations, still the losses continued – two to crashes and two to enemy action – and in late 1916 the surviving members of the fleet were transferred to the navy for anti-submarine work.

With ground operations at a stalemate, French politicians were also turning their eyes to the air, impatient to carry the fight to the enemy rear. Dirigibles alone would clearly not suffice, and over the winter of 1914–15 four bomber *groupes*, each three squadrons strong, were created under the direct command of French headquarters – the Grand Quartier Général (GQG). During the spring and early summer of 1915, GQG experimented with its new force, using the bombers tactically to support its offensive in Artois, and strategically to launch attacks on chemical and explosive works in the Ruhr. These long-distance raids held particular appeal for politicians and press, eager to retaliate against the Germans, but they involved enormous risks. Heavy and slow, French bombers were easy prey for enemy fighters, especially after the Germans gained air superiority that summer. Attempts to fly in mutually protective formations helped a little, as did flying missions at night. By September, however, GQG had suspended all strategic raids in favour of tactical operations, striking directly at the enemy rear in search of battlefield victory in Champagne and Artois.

Throughout the following winter, the situation remained unchanged. Still vulnerable to enemy fighters and AA fire, with too few fighters to protect them (and those fighters diverted to Verdun), the bomber squadrons were divided between the armies, with orders to strike at targets in the immediate enemy rear. Strategic operations resumed in the autumn of 1916, with an Anglo-French raid on the Mauser works at Oberndorf am Neckar, but the screening fighters lacked the range to escort the bomber formation all the way to the target and heavy casualties ensued. The Farman 42 and Breguet-Michelin B.M.4 and B.M.5 proved hopelessly underpowered and vulnerable, while even the Sopwith 1A.2 – the most modern of the aircraft deployed – was virtually obsolete by this stage of the war.

After the Oberndorf disaster, strategic bombing once again came to a halt, limited in 1917 to a handful of token retaliation operations and an under-resourced attempt to blockade German steel supplies from Lorraine and Luxembourg. Early that year, GB1 and GB3 were again switched to tactical work, striking the enemy lines of communication in support of the Chemin des Dames offensive, particularly around Cambrai and Laon. A SPAD escort accompanied the bombers whenever possible, but the disparity in speed between the types made it hard to maintain formation. The fighters were also accused of haring off each time they spotted an opponent on the horizon, however distant he might be. Only late that year, with the introduction of the reliable, powerful Breguet 14, would the bomber force be rejuvenated.

Belfort (Territoire de Belfort), 1915. These two pre-war dirigible hangars are pictured before suffering heavy damage in successive German raids. The *Lieutenant-Chauré* and the *Conté* were based here before the outbreak of war. The *Chauré* never saw action, while on 9 August 1914 the *Conté* (Captain Frugier) was badly damaged by friendly fire on its way back from a raid on German troop trains and never flew again. The hangars were demolished in 1917–18 and the components used to construct a new hangar at the naval airship base at Cuers-Pierrefeu (Var).

(**Opposite, above**) Chalais-Meudon (Hauts-de-Seine), 20 June 1917. Female workers at the balloon service depot attach a bolt-rope to a dirigible. The depot at Chalais-Meudon first opened in 1877, with a factory alongside it. Eleven balloons were produced up to 1920, most seeing service in convoy protection and anti-submarine work in the later years of the war.

(**Above**) Issy-les-Moulineaux (Hauts-de-Seine), 15 June 1918. With its streamlined gondola and yellow envelope, a Chalais-Meudon CM0 to CM4 dirigible manoeuvres above this airfield on the outskirts of Paris. Introduced in 1917, and based at Guipavas (Finistère), the five balloons in the series served on convoy protection duties in the English Channel, but were scrapped just three years later. Issy-les-Moulineaux was a centre of early aviation – the Farman brothers made their first flights there, and it served as the departure point for many pre-war races. It boasted a hangar for Astra-Torres dirigibles, as well as wartime factories for Nieuport and Caudron. After the war, Voisin opened a car factory there. The airfield itself fell into disuse, but still operates as a heliport.

(**Opposite, below**) Near Rethel (Ardennes), October 1916. German soldiers gather around the wreckage of the dirigible *Alsace* (Lieutenant André Cohen). Much larger than previous French designs, the *Alsace* began operations in September 1915. On the clear, moonlit night of 2 October 1916, the craft was raiding Vouziers (Ardennes), an important railway hub on the Champagne front. Flying low for better visibility, the balloon was shot down by German flak. One crew member was killed in the crash landing and his six companions were captured.

(**Above**) Marquise-Rinxent (Pas-de-Calais), 26 May 1918. A Zodiac dirigible lands at this base near Boulogne-sur-Mer, opened in 1916. Two Sea Scout (*SS21* and *SS26*) and five Zodiac craft (*VZ0, VZ1, VZ2, VZ6* and *VZ8*) served here after the dirigibles transferred to the navy. The base saw its final flight in September 1919 and closed two months later. Its then commander, Lieutenant de vaisseau Jacques Trolley de Prévaux (1888–1944), remained in the navy after the war. He and his wife Lotke were later active members of the Resistance, before they were captured, tortured and shot by the Nazis in 1944.

(**Opposite, above**) Off Boulogne-sur-Mer (Pas-de-Calais), 2 April 1917. A Coastal-class dirigible watches over a minesweeping trawler. Over thirty attacks were launched against enemy submarines by the airships of Marquise-Rinxent. They produced no confirmed sinkings, but two bombs dropped by VZ2 (Ensigne de vaisseau Foulletier) inflicted heavy damage on UB119, making it easy prey for two Royal Navy vessels.

(**Opposite, below**) This naval-crewed dirigible is on convoy escort duty. The airships performed particularly important work from 1917 onwards, protecting American convoys arriving in the Breton ports. Operating with a range of 100 to 120 miles, from bases like Guipavas (Finistère) or Paimboeuf (Loire-Atlantique), dirigibles endeavoured to keep the convoy routes clear of mines and submarines. No airship was equipped with wireless; instead each carried a number of carrier pigeons to transmit messages to their base.

(**Opposite, above**) Belfort, February 1915. Pilots and observers are pictured with a Voisin 1. Three squadrons equipped with this type – VB107, VB108, and VB109 – were then forming and would arrive at Belfort over the following months. The man in the fur coat may well be Captain François Glaize (1882–?), CO of VB107 from February 1915. The orginal caption to this photograph describes the group as newly returned from a raid on Freiburg im Breisgau, mounted from Belfort on 18 February 1915. That raid, however, was undertaken by MF14, equipped with the Farman M.F.11.

(**Opposite, below**) Esquennoy (Oise), 2 February 1916. A Voisin 3 of GB3 (VB107, VB108 and VB109) sits outside the Bessonneau hangars. The Voisin, in all its variants, was the workhorse of French bomber squadrons deep into the war. With its metal construction and reliable Canton-Unné engine, it could carry a decent payload for its era, at a good altitude, and was built in quantity by sub-contractors Breguet, Esnault-Pelterie and Nieuport. Like many early aircraft, however, it struggled from mid-1915 onwards, proving too slow when matched against the newer German fighters.

(**Above**) Lunéville (Meurthe-et-Moselle), September 1915. Bombs are removed from the underground bomb store. For safety's sake, this was situated far from the hangars and accommodation. Until the final months of the war, all bombs were modified artillery shells: the 50kg bomb (left) was manufactured from a 155mm shell; the 10kg bombs lined up (right), from 90mm shells. Two of the 10kg bombs are designed as anti-personnel fragmentation devices.

Lunéville (Meurthe-et-Moselle), September 1915. Very carefully, ground crew manoeuvre a 100kg bomb from a lorry before loading it beneath a waiting Farman. The bomb was made from a 220mm shell, modified by the addition of fins. In October 1916, mechanic Claude Coupade was serving with F25, then flying night bombing missions from Vadelaincourt (Meuse): 'The bombs are made of heavy-gauge metal, with a sealed chamber filled with a liquid that gives off yellow fumes in contact with the air. A second liquid is introduced into the bomb just before it is set in the rack; that's when it becomes dangerous.' Unsurprisingly, accidents happened. 'Some pals were placing their bombs beneath the plane, when they dropped one and the chamber burst. The liquid seeping from the joints was set alight by a lantern. It exploded while they were smothering it with earth. One mechanic died, another lost a leg, and everyone nearby was injured.'

Eugène Gilbert (1889–1918). Gilbert (MS23/49) was a prominent pre-war racer, who flew Sommer or Morane aircraft to success in the Gordon Bennett, Pommery and Michelin trophies before joining MS23 on the outbreak of war. On 27 June 1915 he was interned in Switzerland, forced down by engine problems while returning from a raid on the Zeppelin sheds at Friedrichshafen. He escaped in May 1916, only to be returned by the French authorities for breaking his parole, but escaped again a month later. He became a test pilot for Gnôme engines, but was killed in a flying accident on 16 May 1918.

Vadelaincourt (Meuse), 1916. Captain Louis Robert de Beauchamp (1887–1916), CO of N23, chats to some of his pilots. N23 was operating a mixture of aircraft: Nieuport 11 and Nieuport 16 fighters, and Nieuport 10 and Sopwith 1A.2 reconnaissance machines. Beauchamp had made his name in the Sopwith, flying impromptu bombing raids on Essen on 2 September 1915, and on Munich two months later. He was shot down and killed in a SPAD 7 over Fort Vaux on 17 December 1916.

This pilot and observer are well wrapped-up against the chill. Goggles protect the eyes, while the observer wears a leather face mask to ward off the icy winds of the slipstream. 'I've never been so cold in my life,' complained André Quennehen (MF5), after a raid in February 1916. 'I couldn't get out of the plane when I landed. My legs and feet were completely numb.'

Above Breteuil (Oise), 24 December 1916. Taken from the observer's seat, this image shows how the engine and tail assembly of the Voisin restricted the view over its vulnerable rear, a blind spot readily exploited by enemy fighters.

Caught in the spotlight, a Caudron prepares to take off on a night mission. With no special training or navigational equipment, pilots had to rely on dead reckoning to find their goal. 'We'd precious little training when you think about it,' recalled Major Paul Gignoux (VB101). 'I took off on my first night raid with a total of just fifty-three hours' flying time … The target is often lit up and quite distinctive: a station, a railway line, a factory. Ability to see the ground comes with experience.'

(**Opposite, above**) Lunéville (Meurthe-et-Moselle), September 1915. Fully bombed up, a Farman M.F.11 prepares for take-off. The bombs here are modified 90mm shells; the top row are all fragmentation bombs. A lot of early defensive armament was extemporized by the squadrons. Mounted on this aircraft is an 1895 Colt machine gun, its ammunition belt placed in the curved bracket above the pilot's head. The gun was used in small numbers but was unpopular with aircrew because it tended to jam.

(**Opposite, below**) Savy-Berlette (Pas-de-Calais), February 1916. A Voisin 4 of VC113 leaves the airfield. First introduced in late summer 1915, the Voisin 4 was simply a renumbered Voisin 3 armed with a 37mm gun. Formed into special *sections d'avions-canons* (SAC), it was intended to perform in a variety of roles: fighter, ground attack and bomber protection. In practice, the type was too slow for fighter or escort duties, but it proved useful in attacking enemy searchlight and flak positions and continued in service until early 1917. VC113 was formed in September 1915 by amalgamating SAC6 and SAC7.

(**Above**) Belrain-Rumont (Marne), January 1918. A Voisin 8 of VB114 attracts a crowd at the airfield. Introduced into squadron service in 1916, the Voisin 8 was one of a number of vain attempts to make incremental improvements to the type. Streamlining the fuselage of the Voisin 3 and adding a 150hp Salmson engine had first produced the Voisin 5. When the Salmson proved a failure, a more powerful 220hp Peugot engine was tried instead, and the type was renumbered as the Voisin 8. But its performance was poor, the new engine unreliable, and within months it was being phased out. The Voisin 8 was also equipped as a night bomber, the cluster of lights on the nose serving to illuminate the ground during take-off and landing, as well as to flash identification signals to ground units.

(**Opposite, above**) Le Bourget (Seine-Saint-Denis). A Breguet Michelin B.M.2 stands outside a hangar. The B.M.2 was the first Breguet-Michelin to enter service, in September 1915, equipping bomber *groupe* BM1, which united three squadrons – BM117, BM118 and BM119. Its original underpowered, unreliable Canton-Unné engine was replaced by a Renault to good effect. Yet like the Voisin it was designed to replace, the B.M.2 was slow and vulnerable to fighters and soon restricted to night operations only.

(**Opposite, below**) Romagny-sous-Rougemont (Territoire de Belfort), February 1917. A Sopwith 1A.2 of SOP7 prepares for take-off. The Sopwith 1A.2 was the redesignated Sopwith 1½-Strutter, initially bought in small numbers from the British and then manufactured under licence. Although superior to its outdated Farman predecessors, the Sopwith too was virtually obsolete by the time it reached the front. Attached to VI Corps, SOP7 was about to leave the Vosges for the Chemin des Dames. Three months later, the squadron was the first to receive the new Breguet 14.

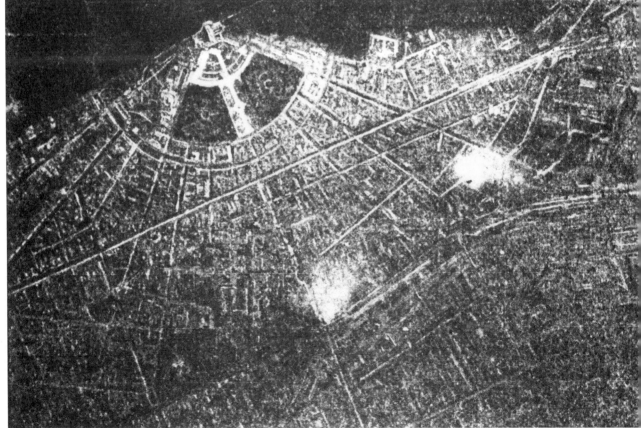

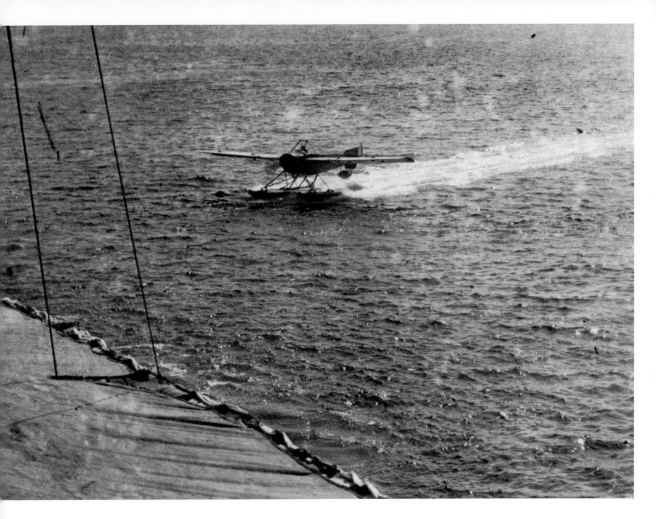

(**Opposite, above**) Bombs fall on a target near Metz (Moselle). Metz had been the target of Cesari and Prudhommeaux's raid on the Zeppelin sheds in August 1914, of the first night raid in February 1915 and, as a vital communications hub and garrison town, remained a permanent objective thereafter. Over four years of war, the city endured 138 raids, with civilian casualties (according to one source) amounting to over 100 dead and 300 injured.

(**Opposite, below**) The Karlsruhe raid, 22 June 1916. Led by Captain Henri de Kérillis (1889–1958), the aircraft of C66 bombed Karlsruhe after the recent death of French civilians in an enemy raid on Bar-le-Duc (Meuse), home town of President Raymond Poincaré (1860–1934). The French bombers were targeting the railway station, but instead hit a circus during a performance: 117 people were killed and 152 injured. While castigating the Zeppelin as a simple weapon of terror, de Kérillis thought his own action justified: 'Fifty Sopwiths dropping five hundred bombs will have strewn enough German guts across the streets of the town to give food for thought to the burners of Reims and the sinkers of the *Lusitania*.'

(**Above**) A Nieuport 6H float-plane approaches its parent ship for recovery, c.1916. The navy had quickly recognized the potential of aircraft to strike against the enemy and developed its own range of specialized types capable of operating over the sea. A flight of six aircraft based in the Adriatic around the seaplane carrier *La Foudre* proved ineffective against the Austrians in 1914, but after transferring to Port Said (Egypt) in 1915 they performed useful reconnaissance duties against the Turks, operating from the seaplane carriers *Anne* and *Raven II*, and from British vessels HMS *Minerva*, HMS *Doris* and HMINS *Hardinge*.

(**Opposite, above**) Dunkerque (Nord), December 1915. An FBA Type C seaplane is launched from the base here. Opened by the navy in December 1914, the base also included a satellite airfield at Saint-Pol-sur-Mer. The seaplanes patrolled an area westwards as far as Gravelines (Nord), and north-westwards to the Nord Hinder light-vessel. In the background are some of the Royal Navy ships tasked with bombarding the German-held coast, including the monitors HMS *Prince Eugene* and HMS *General Wolfe*.

(**Opposite, below**) Saint-Raphaël (Var). An FBA Type C seaplane in difficulties receives a tow back to base. The type saw extensive service in land-based patrol and anti-submarine work. Although progressively replaced by the more powerful Type H from May 1916, it continued in service until spring 1917. The base at Saint-Raphaël housed the first naval flying school, created in 1912. Originally equipped with twelve Nieuport float planes, by 1917 it comprised twenty-four FBAs, eighteen Donner-Denhauts, eight Telliers and four Caudron G4s, providing basic training to pilots and observers, as well as advanced training for aspirant fighter pilots.

(**Above**) Dunkerque (Nord), February 1917. Aircrew wait as their FBA Type H is lowered into the water for take-off. Engaged largely on anti-submarine patrols, the French seaplanes suffered in clashes with their German counterparts and from mid-1917 required one or more Hanriot HD2s as escorts. Seaplanes took off and landed via a long approach across the entire width of the harbour, between the quays and the Eastern Mole. The basin was shared with a British seaplane base, located behind the photographer.

(**Above**) De Panne (West-Vlaanderen). In addition to flying boats, the naval air base at Dunkerque (Nord) also maintained separate flights of Nieuport fighters and Voisin bombers at its satellite airfield at Saint-Pol-sur-Mer. Here, one of the bomber flight, a notoriously unreliable Voisin 8, has been forced down on the beach with engine failure.

(**Opposite, above**) Zeebrugge (West-Vlaanderen). This aerial view of the German-held port shows the harbour and the mouth of the canal leading inland to Bruges. As the hub of a canal network with several exits to the sea, Bruges was a major centre of U-boat activity throughout the war. Various unsuccessful attempts were made to bomb and shell the canal mouths, culminating in the British Zeebrugge raid of 23 April 1918.

(**Opposite, below**) Ostend (West-Vlaanderen). Like Zeebrugge, occupied Ostend lay at the mouth of an important canal network providing shelter and repair facilities for U-boats. The British made several attempts to block the harbour: in 1915 and 1917, when monitors tried to destroy the lock gates by bombardment, then again in April and May 1918.

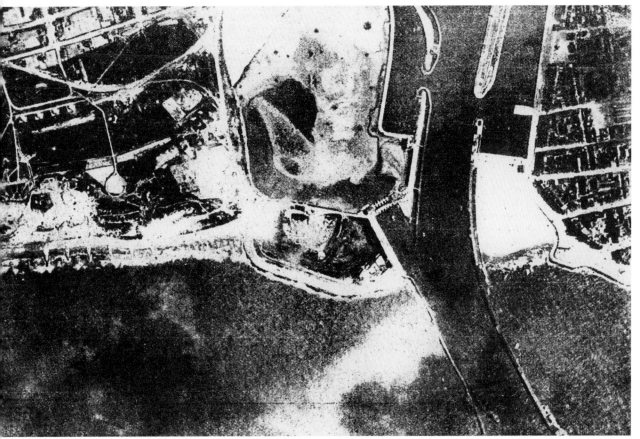

Chapter Four

The crucible of the service

Research conducted at Vincennes into means of arming aircraft was still ongoing in August 1914. Charles de Rose and Roland Garros had identified the way forward: take a fast aircraft and fit a machine gun firing forward through the arc of the propeller. Yet the underlying problem remained: how to stop the bullets hitting the propeller blades, imperilling both aircraft and crew. Garros developed the idea of equipping each blade with a deflector plate and, in his modified Morane-Saulnier Type L single-seater, shot down three enemy machines in early April 1915. That same month, however, he was forced down and captured behind enemy lines near Kortrijk (West-Vlaanderen).

In Germany, manufacturer Anthony Fokker had perfected a different technique, developing a synchronizer gear that used the turning of the propeller to control the firing of a Maxim gun. Thus equipped, the new Fokker Eindecker gave the Germans several months of uncontested air superiority in mid-1915, and by the end of the year the French squadrons were in crisis, their obsolescent Caudron, Farman and Voisin types increasingly vulnerable and unable to operate without escorts, and those escorts in turn outclassed by the Fokker.

Meanwhile, as aviation commander of Fifth Army, de Rose was determined to win over the sceptics by demonstrating that aircraft were capable of seeking out the enemy, then pursuing, catching and destroying him. In March 1915, at Jonchery-sur-Vesle (Marne), he took one of his two seater-reconnaissance units, replaced the Nieuport 6M with six new Morane-Saulnier Type L Parasol two-seater monoplanes, the only contemporary French aircraft faster than its opponents, hand-picked his pilots and turned N12 into France's first fighter squadron, MS12. The crews were still armed with just a four-round carbine, so pilots were instructed to make surprise attacks, flying high and hiding in cloud or sun before swooping down on the enemy, close enough to give the observer the chance for a head shot.

Five victories were gained in April alone, but the Parasol's rotary engine made it notoriously difficult to fly, effectively excluding all but the most experienced pilots. De Rose knew what he really needed was a specialist single-seater, and in June 1915 he opted for the smaller Nieuport 11 – nicknamed the 'Bébé' – a fast, highly manoeuvrable, lightweight model developed from pre-war competition racers. He worked with the company to modify the original design, particularly to reduce the excessive engine vibration, and also abandoned Garros's heavy deflector plates – now revealed to cut airspeed as well as compromising the propeller's aerodynamic performance. An MS12 mechanic, Sergeant Robert Alkan, was working to perfect a synchronizer gear to match the Fokker system, but in the interim de Rose had a Hotchkiss or Lewis machine gun fixed to the upper wing, to fire over, rather than through, the arc of the propeller. Each plane carried three 25-round drums or strips for the Hotchkiss, or three 47-round drums for the Lewis; reloading, however, was a tricky business that put both pilot and plane out of action for a dangerously long time.

With the Nieuport Bébé slowly reaching the front line, serving initially alongside the older Nieuport 10 two-seaters, France had its first specialist fighter aircraft, superior to the rival Eindecker in speed, manoeuvrability and rate-of-climb. The early Bébé was still outgunned – but in February 1916 Alkan successfully synchronized a belt-fed Vickers machine gun, at last redressing the balance in firepower and eliminating the need to change magazines in mid-combat. The Vickers made its debut on the front in May 1916 and quickly became the standard weapon of the Bébé and its successors.

On arriving at the front, the first Bébés were assigned a dual role: defending the skies above Nancy and escorting the vulnerable bomber *groupes*. Fighter strategy, however, remained in flux. Some senior officers favoured distributing the new machines among the army, army corps and bomber squadrons to provide close protection. But de Rose and Major Édouard Barès, GQG's aviation commander, held the opposite view: they advocated concentrating fighter resources by combining several squadrons under a single command. They were also evolving ideas of 'indirect protection', providing the cooperation squadrons with a safety zone on either side of the battlefront by sending fighters across the lines to destroy enemy machines. Operating over German-held territory would be a risky affair, forcing pilots to nurse their planes home against the prevailing south-westerlies, while constantly exposed to aerial attack and hostile ground fire. Inevitably, French losses would be high; but, they argued, those suffered by the enemy would be greater still.

The surprise German attack at Verdun on 21 February 2016 gave the pair the opportunity to implement their plans. In the crisis, General Pétain turned to de Rose, offering him *carte blanche* to wrest back air superiority over the battlefield – and in the process create France's first independent fighter wing. Within days, de Rose had combined six all-fighter squadrons – N15, N37, N57, N65, N67 and N69 – in a provisional *groupement* under his command. Over the vehement protests of senior commanders, he then commandeered all the best pilots, including such notable fliers as Guynemer, Brocard, Navarre, Nungesser and Deullin. Equipping them with the Nieuport 11, he based them at airfields south-west of Verdun, including Issoncourt,

Vadelaincourt and Souilly, and finally despatched them across the lines to a depth of 5 or 6km in formations three, six or even nine-aircraft strong.

On 21 March, de Rose's critics regained the upper hand: the *groupement* was disbanded and the squadrons dispersed across the Verdun front. Within a week, however, they had been reunited, now under the command of Captain Auguste Le Révérend (MS23). De Rose had been kicked upstairs, reluctantly agreeing to replace Barès at GQG, but he died before he could take up his new post, killed while demonstrating the Nieuport Bébé on 11 May 1916.

The battle of Verdun was the turning point for military aviation. For the first time, gaining air superiority formed a key component of French and German strategy; air power played a major, continuous part in the action; and the value of a specialist fighter formation was amply proven. It was, said General Pétain, 'the crucible in which the French air service was forged'. In April 1916, a new six-squadron *groupement*, based at Cachy, near Amiens, was created for the forthcoming Somme offensive, and from 1 July French fighters flying in powerful formations swept the enemy from the sky. The tactics so successfully employed at Verdun proved equally effective here, while the arrival of planes like the Nieuport 11, Nieuport 17 and a superior new type, the SPAD 7 – all fitted with a synchronized Vickers machine gun – finally allowed the French to start matching German firepower.

Caught unaware by this concentration of French aircraft, the Germans could summon little in immediate response. Yet air superiority could never be permanent or absolute. Any technical, tactical or organizational innovation would provoke a response, while even a weaker opponent could pose a threat by concentrating aerial resources to achieve local superiority, conducting front-line reconnaissance, spotting and oblique photography missions at low altitude over home territory or penetrating the enemy lines with a surprise solo attack. In late summer 1916 the Germans recovered air parity, transferring squadrons from Verdun and despatching new types to the front, just as the SPAD 7 was beset by teething troubles. A new German specialist fighter, the Albatros D.III, was deployed in a new formation, the elite Jasta, each five to ten machines strong. And, in Jasta 2, Captain Oswald Boelcke followed the French lead by assembling some of the best pilots in the service, among them Erwin Boehme, Hans Reimann and Manfred von Richthofen.

In September 1916, General Joffre gave permanent status to his fighter *groupements*. In October and November he went further, creating three fighter *groupes* – GC11, GC12 (the former Groupement de Cachy) and GC13 – all under the direct command of GQG. Employing de Rose's system of permanent patrols, the *groupes* were given a dual mission – to secure control of the skies by engaging enemy fighters, attacking balloons and conducting long-range reconnaissance missions, and to hunt targets of opportunity on the ground. Air superiority was Joffre's main priority, now considered vital to operational success. To achieve these objectives, the French not only needed more and better aircraft, but also new tactics. Boelcke had spent the summer of 1916 devising sophisticated collective manoeuvring techniques for the new German Jastas, and the French struggled to find a response. After patrols two aircraft strong proved a failure, full squadrons were despatched to range deep over the lines on the Chemin des Dames in April 1917. But these, too, were ineffective – sweeps of such size were easily spotted, and avoided, by the enemy – and the French eventually settled on four-man patrols, flying SPADs.

Meanwhile the men who flew the fighters had become celebrities. In their boldly marked aircraft, the successes of pilots and squadrons could be presented as 'victories' in an otherwise sterile campaign and served a useful role in moulding public opinion. Newspapers and magazines, particularly Jacques Mortane's *La Guerre Aérienne Illustrée*, borrowed the sporting term 'ace', and the usage was officially adopted for any pilot who obtained five or more victories (ten from 1918).

Adolphe Pégoud (1889–1915), standing. Pégoud (MF25/MS37/49) was a pre-war Blériot test pilot, the first man to jump by parachute from a plane, and among the first to loop-the-loop. He was also the first French air ace: in February 1915, serving with MF25, he became the hero of the hour after shooting down two aircraft and forcing down a third, all in a single day. He was credited with a total of six confirmed victories before he was shot down and killed on 31 August 1915. Seated in the car, a Vinot-Deguigand, is Soldier Monternier, one of Pégoud's two mechanics. The car was presented to the ace by its manufacturer; Pégoud would not be the last flyer to be showered with gifts of this kind.

(**Above**) Near Gueux (Marne), May 1915. The forced landing of this Morane-Saulnier Type L Parasol has attracted quite a crowd. Initially used as a light bomber/reconnaissance machine, the Parasol was fast and manoeuvrable, with a high wing allowing pilot and observer excellent downward vision, but its lack of forward-firing armament severely limited its effectiveness as a fighter. The Parasols of MS37 engaged enemy aircraft several times that summer – all without success. As a fighter, the type soon gave way to the Nieuport 11 'Bébé'.

(**Opposite, above**) Rosnay (Marne), September 1915. Aircraft of MS12 are pictured outside their hangars. In the background are three Morane-Saulnier LA Parasols, while (front right) is a Nieuport 10, the forerunner of the Nieuport 11 Bébé. The Voisin 3 (left) may be a visitor from a neighbouring squadron. Using the speed of the Parasol to gain advantage over the enemy, Major Charles de Rose had recently transformed MS12 into France's first fighter squadron. The idiosyncrasies of the type's rotary engine, however, soon persuaded him to turn instead to Nieuports.

(**Opposite, below**) Vadelaincourt (Meuse), May 1916. A Nieuport Bébé of N3 is refuelled by hand. The Bébé was a much better plane than the Parasol, with far fewer vices. This aircraft, *N871*, is believed to have been flown by Sergeant André Chainat (1892–1961; B4/MS23/38/ N/SPA3) and Sous-lieutenant Jean Subervie (1891–1916; VB110/N69). Its machine gun is mounted on the upper wing, the temporary expedient adopted by de Rose while Sergeant Alkan perfected his synchronizer gear.

(**Above**) Minaucourt (Marne), March 1916. Left to right are three 'likely lads': Sous-lieutenant Georges 'Pivolo' Pelletier d'Oisy (1892–1953), Sergeant Jean Navarre (1895–1919) and Maurice Tabuteau (1884–1976). Pelletier d'Oisy (HF19/MS12/N69) joined the aviation service in 1912 and retired as a general; he was credited with five confirmed victories. Navarre (MF8/MS12/N67) was an excellent flier, with twelve confirmed victories, whose indiscipline made him the despair of his COs. Tabuteau was a pre-war record-breaker. After one accident too many, he retired from aviation on the grounds that it was 'too dangerous' and took up motor racing instead! On the outbreak of war, he put his flying skills to good use as a test pilot.

(**Opposite**) Over Verdun (Meuse), July 1916. These two Nieuport fighters are escorting a Farman of MF33, whose observer Lieutenant Nissim de Camondo has taken this photograph. The badge on the fuselage of the nearer of the pair – a bird of prey in gold on a pennant of red and brown – suggests that it belongs to N67. Based at Froidos (Meuse), N67 formed part of de Rose's elite *groupement* and included among its pilots Sergeant Jean Navarre.

(**Above**) Lemmes (Meuse), May 1916. Sergeant Jean Navarre climbs into his red-painted Nieuport 16. Serving with N67 over Verdun, Navarre had painted his first Nieuport in red, white and blue stripes; his second was given a tricolour pennant on its side, while his third – and the only one armed with a synchronized forward-firing gun – was all red. He claimed that the colour was chosen simply to lure his German opponents. 'He'll be something special,' commented Roland Garros wryly. 'That's if he doesn't kill himself first.'

(**Opposite, above**) Malzéville (Meurthe-et-Moselle), May 1916. *N828*, a Nieuport 12 of N102, prepares for take-off. The type was an improved version of the Nieuport 10 and speedy enough to operate alongside the Bébés of the famous Groupement de Cachy, later GC12. On 23 January 1917, with N102 based at Sacy-le-Grand (Oise), this machine suffered mechanical difficulties. It was forced down behind German lines and its pilot, Maréchal des logis François de Lévis-Mirepoix (1894–?), taken prisoner.

(**Opposite, below**) Vadelaincourt (Meuse), 9 October 1916. Adjudant Maxime Lenoir (1888–1916) poses in front of his SPAD 7. Famed for his pre-war aerobatic displays, Lenoir (C18/N23) had been posted to the cavalry on mobilization and obtained his transfer to aviation only with great difficulty. Posted to N23, he was credited with eleven confirmed victories, mostly around Verdun, before he was shot down and killed on 25 October 1916. 'I didn't call my plane *Trompe la mort* [Death Defier] for nothing,' he claimed. 'I scoff at death. It doesn't scare me. Life can be sweet, but a good death is no less fine.'

(**Above**) Cachy (Somme), 15 September 1916. Lieutenant Georges Guynemer (1894–1917) is pictured (left) with his two mechanics and his SPAD 7, *Le Vieux Charles*. With fifty-three confirmed victories to his name, Guynemer (N/SPA3) was the most celebrated French pilot of the war. He was killed in action over Poelkapelle (West-Vlaanderen) on 11 September 1917; his body was never recovered. He had served as a mechanic before qualifying as a pilot, and later used his technical skills to tinker with his machine in search of small but vital improvements in performance. The modern Armée de l'Air base at Dijon-Longvic (Côte d'Or) is named in his honour.

(**Opposite, above**) Le Hamel (Somme), 1916. Lieutenant Georges Guynemer and his SPAD 7 draw the crowds again. Guynemer eventually tired of all the adulation. One contemporary spotted the ace on leave in Paris shortly before his death: 'The Parisians recognized him. How could they not, when his picture was in all the papers? On the *grands boulevards*, the locals fell silent when he passed. They almost came to a halt. I followed him for a time. He was slightly stooped, tired of giving his all, marked out by death.'

(**Opposite, below**) Ferme de la Bonne Maison (Marne), 5 July 1917. Lieutenant Georges Guynemer shows off his SPAD 12 to General Louis Franchet d'Espèrey, GOC Northern Army Group. Although a significant improvement on the Nieuport 11, the SPAD 7 was still under-armed, with a single machine gun. Guynemer decided to fit an additional 37mm cannon, firing through the hollow hub of the propeller, and the result was the SPAD 12. The ace scored two victories in the type, but its performance was hampered by the weight of the gun, while the breech protruded into the cockpit, preventing the use of a conventional control column. The SPAD 12 was confined to experienced pilots only, and just a handful were ever manufactured.

De Panne (West-Vlaanderen), 26 May 1917. Lieutenant Charles Nungesser (1892–1927) lands his Nieuport 17 on the beach, close to Belgian Army HQ. The unexpected arrival of the ace quickly drew a crowd of eager onlookers, including the head of the British Military Mission to the Belgians, Prince Alexander of Teck, Earl of Athlone (left). The oft-injured Nungesser (V106/116/N/SPA65) was eventually credited with forty-three confirmed victories, in the process breaking almost every major bone in his body. He died in 1927, lost with Captain François Coli (N/SPA62) while attempting to cross the Atlantic.

Lieutenant Paul Tarascon (1882–1977). Tarascon (N3/31/SPA62) had lost a foot in a crash landing while learning to fly in 1911. Nevertheless, he volunteered for aviation in August 1914 and was eventually credited with twelve confirmed victories. In 1923, Tarascon was badly burned in another accident, forcing him to abandon plans to join his old SPA62 comrade François Coli in attempting an Atlantic crossing; his place on the ill-fated flight was taken by Charles Nungesser.

Lieutenant Georges Madon (1892–1924). After escaping from captivity following a forced landing in Switzerland, Madon (BL30/MF218/N/SPA38) was eventually credited with forty-one confirmed victories. A man whose prickly temperament made him more respected than liked, he flew an aircraft painted red in homage to Jean Navarre. The sector commander would allow no more than a red stripe around the fuselage, but this was gradually and surreptitiously widened by Madon's mechanic until it covered the entire body. Madon survived the war, but died in his native Bizerta (Tunisia) during a flying display organized to celebrate the anniversary of the armistice and the inauguration of a memorial to Roland Garros.

Cachy (Somme), 30 September 1916. Adjudant René Dorme (1894–1917) poses with his Nieuport 17. Dorme had transferred to aviation from the artillery in 1915, serving with C94 and N95 before joining the prestigious N3 in May 1916. A skilled pilot, he vied with Guynemer to be the leading ace and was eventually credited with twenty-three confirmed victories. He was shot down over Reims on 25 May 1917. The modern Armée de l'Air base at Villacoublay (Yvelines) is named in his honour.

(**Above**) Near Montagne-Fayel (Somme), 18 May 1918. Captain Albert Deullin (1890–1923) poses with his SPAD 7. Deullin (MS62/MS/N3/SPA73) had transferred to aviation from the cavalry. Appointed CO of SPA73 in February 1917, and commander of GC19 (SPA73, SPA85, SPA95 and SPA96) in 1918, he was eventually credited with twenty confirmed victories. Deullin was also a profound tactical thinker, whose analyses contributed greatly to the fighter tactics evolved by the French air service in 1917–18. He became a test pilot after the war, dying in a crash at Villacoublay (Yvelines) in 1923.

(**Opposite, above**) Summer 1916. This Nieuport 16, *Alfred*, flown by Sergeant Marcel Garet (MF40/N67/23), is equipped with Le Prieur anti-balloon rockets. One role of the fighters was to deny intelligence-gathering capability to the enemy, and Lieutenant de Vaisseau Yves le Prieur had designed his rocket to down static balloons by igniting the gas in the envelope. The weapon was attached to the inter-plane struts of an aircraft and was fired electrically, with a range of around 200m. It made its debut in May 1916, but though spectacular proved inaccurate in action. Garet died in a mid-air collision over Vadelaincourt (Meuse) on 2 July 1916, closing with Leutnant Werner Neuhaus (FA203) to fire at point-blank range. Both men were killed in the incident.

(**Opposite, below**) Sainte-Ménehould (Marne), May 1916. Sergeant Henri Barnay (1891–1944) relishes the prospect of a glass of champagne in the mess. Barnay transferred to aviation from the engineers in 1915, serving first with MS98T in the Dardanelles. He was invalided home, joining N37 in January 1916. After losing six teeth in an air accident that July, he was later reduced in rank and returned to the engineers, ending the war in tanks. As proprietor of a hotel/restaurant in Pagny-sur-Moselle (Meurthe-et-Moselle), Barnay was deported in 1944 for aiding escaped prisoners and died in captivity at the Neuengamme camp, near Hamburg.

Chaudun (Aisne), 27 May 1917. The men of SPA65 enjoy a break from routine, courtesy of a troupe of entertainers from the Théâtre aux Armées de la République, recently arrived at the airfield to put on a show in a hangar. Conceived by Émile Fabre, administrator of the Comédie Française, and journalist and theatrical director Alphonse Séché, the Théâtre blended professional artistes and enthusiastic soldiers of varying degrees of talent. Between February 1916 and September 1919, they staged over 1,100 shows in front of some 1.5 million spectators. Not every audience was appreciative: one 'star' admitted giving 'a pretty mediocre performance for the indifferent *poilus* ... The dour, plodding northerners chewed on pieces of straw, while those in the front row smiled uncomprehendingly.'

Art-sur-Meurthe (Meurthe-et-Moselle), 1917. Pilot Octave Lapize (1887–1917) zeroes in the guns of his Nieuport 17. Lapize (N54/90) was a racing cyclist, winner of the 1910 Tour de France, and French national champion from 1910 to 1913. He transferred to aviation from transport in 1915, qualifying as a pilot in February 1917, but was shot down and killed on 14 July 1917 while attacking a German two-seater over Flirey (Meurthe-et-Moselle).

Corbeaulieu (Oise), March 1917. Mechanics of N102 watch as a pilot prepares for take-off in this SPAD, *S239*. The squadron badge of N102 – a light blue disc with yellow rays – adorns the aircraft in the foreground; the letters LN on the tail represent the personal mark of an anonymous pilot. If our pilot was hoping to fly this machine, he is doomed to disappointment: the propeller has been removed for maintenance!

Cachy (Somme), 10 September 1916. Mechanics of SPA3 load an ammunition belt into a SPAD. The most successful pilots were perfectionists, checking their own ammunition to prevent a misfire or jam in mid-dogfight. Albert Deullin applauded their caution. 'The fighter pilot must be his own armourer,' he counselled. 'He must know his weapon inside and out, care for it as he does his engine, check its condition and maintenance daily, watch the belts being loaded, learn to recognize all types of jam and how to avoid them as well as clear them quickly in the air. Many men have tried to neglect this fundamental principle. All have regretted it.'

Chapter Five

Gothas by day, Zeppelins by night

The first enemy air raid on Paris arrived at 12.45pm on 30 August 1914, when a Taube dropped five bombs from a height of 1,000m, killing one and wounding four, before flying off untouched by the guns of the CRP. Four armed Farmans were immediately despatched to reinforce the defenders of the capital, but to no effect; the raids continued over the next three months, killing eleven and wounding fifty. One Farman got within range of an intruder on 2 September, but its machine gun jammed on the tenth round and the German escaped unharmed.

Enemy aircraft, limited in range, had to follow the shortest route to their target, so could only attack from the north or north-east. Zeppelins, however, had the reach to threaten from any direction. General Gallieni, commanding the CRP, favoured mobile motorized AA units to counter the danger, but a shortage of vehicles stymied his plans. Instead, he established an outer ring of listening posts some 100km from Paris, with fifteen fixed batteries – each deploying field guns, machine guns and searchlights – set in an inner ring on the likeliest approach routes to the capital. As soon as the alert was sounded, a city-wide blackout would follow.

Reinforced by an additional line of listening posts placed in an arc some 20km north and east of Paris, these dispositions remained untested until 21 March 1915, when two Zeppelins bombed the city to little effect. The early warning system worked well enough; less so the guns, which struggled to find the right range and tended to fire indiscriminately. An extra seventeen planes were added to the CRP strength, but when the Germans returned on 28 May 1915 not one machine left the ground. Standing patrols were introduced in response, but they too were ineffective: ground-to-air communications were reliant on rudimentary cloth panels; messages could be delayed by up to an hour between listening post and airfield; and the newer, more powerful aircraft types were routinely allocated to the front line. In consequence, the pilots of the CRP seldom had time to reach interception height before the enemy flew off.

Attacking in heavy fog, the Germans penetrated the defences twice more, on 29 and 30 January 1916. Twenty-six French aircraft braved the conditions that first night: five spotted the intruder, but none was capable of matching its height or speed. The following night a dozen planes went up, but the fog was denser still, forcing them back to the airfield. Night flying remained a skill acquired through experience and possessed only by a handful of pilots; the first dedicated school did not open until November 1918.

In the final year of the war, enemy attacks on Paris resumed with a vengeance. Between January and September 1918, German bombers – termed 'Gothas', whatever their make – flew 483 separate sorties over the capital. Extra weapons, sound locators and searchlights now reinforced the defences, eleven victories were claimed, and the intense barrage deflected over 90 per cent of the raids before they reached the city centre. Many intruders were persuaded to drop their bombs instead on the heavily industrialized northern suburbs. The French hailed this as a moral victory, but numerous factories suffered significant damage, as did the important railway junction at Creil (Oise).

On 23 March 1918, the Germans also opened up with the 'Paris Gun', the so-called 'Big Bertha' – actually two weapons, both 210mm railway-mounted cannon, initially based 121km from the capital, near Crépy-en-Laonnois (Aisne). The first shell landed at 7.15am in the Place de la République; the second, fifteen minutes later, in the Rue Charles V; and a third in the Boulevard de Strasbourg. Over the next twenty-four hours, twenty-one shells landed in the city proper, and one in Châtillon (Hauts-de-Seine). The French at first believed themselves under attack from the air: only by reassembling the shell fragments did the truth become apparent. Sound location gave the approximate position of the guns, quickly confirmed by the aircraft of SPA62, and French counter-battery work began immediately – but to little avail. Lying deep within woods, the site was protected by a smokescreen as well as anti-aircraft guns. French artillery and bombers were unable to halt the attacks, and a total of 367 shells landed on Paris between 23 March and 9 August 1918. Only the Allied advance during the second battle of the Marne in July 1918 eventually prompted the Germans to withdraw the massive weapons out of range.

(**Above**) Paris, 11 October 1914. Bemused onlookers gather outside the cathedral of Notre-Dame to watch a German Taube manoeuvre overhead. Two aircraft bombed the city that day, killing four and wounding twenty-eight. Most of the bombs fell around the Gare du Nord and Gare de l'Est, but at least three fell close to the cathedral on the Île de la Cité, right in the heart of the capital.

(**Opposite**) Ferme des Cochets, near Arpajon (Essonne), September 1915. One observation post was established on the roof of these farm buildings, south of the city. From November 1914, command of the capital's anti-aircraft defences was entrusted to naval officers. Capitaine de vaisseau Alphonse Morache (1865–1925) left in 1915 for the battleship *Le Gaulois*, while his successor Capitaine de vaisseau Paul Prère (1867–1915) died soon after taking up his new post. Command finally devolved to Capitaine de frégate Camille Mortenol (1859–1930), the son of a former slave from Guadeloupe. Mortenol was due to retire in 1917, but his service was extended, with the rank and seniority of a colonel in the artillery.

(**Above**) Les Vieux Moulins, Sannois (Val d'Oise), August 1915. Another listening post was set up at these mills situated on high ground north-west of Paris. In more peaceful times, this was a popular spot for day-trippers, celebrated in a *chansonnette* of 1880 by Armand Victorin. Every observation post was equipped with a telephone or sited near a telephone box. Although dedicated exchanges were provided within CRP headquarters, the system had to rely on the public network, which did not always respond quickly enough for military needs.

(**Opposite**) Frépillon (Val d'Oise), August 1915. This Sagnac sound locator is sited at an AA post north-west of Paris. The sound of aircraft engines is collected by its four horns, then fed to the operator via a stethoscope-style pair of earphones. While these devices helped to fix the direction of incoming enemy aircraft, they could do little to determine altitude. Most AA fire was thus too low. Only in mid-1917 did the French artillery discover the operational height of the German bombers – 3,000m – with a subsequent improvement in the accuracy of the guns.

(**Above**) Rue Lapelletier, Paris, 6 October 1917. An experimental hand-held siren powered by compressed air is operated from the roof of the Equitable Life Assurance Company of the United States. Normally sounded by sirens, but sometimes by fire engines or even buglers, the alert was accompanied by a city-wide 'lights out'.

(**Opposite**) Place Pigalle, Paris, 21 February 1918. Metro stations were often used as temporary air-raid shelters, but they were not invulnerable. On the night of 29–30 January 1916, bombs from a Zeppelin penetrated a tunnel on the Boulevard de Belleville, with several casualties; fourteen months later, a Gotha raid on 11 March 1918 hit Bolivar station in the 9th *arrondissement*, killing sixty and injuring thirty-one.

(**Above**) Frépillon (Val d'Oise), 21 March 1915. The searchlight at the Frépillon post scans the skies on the night of the first Zeppelin raid on Paris. It is operated by naval personnel, who had been among the first to arrive to defend the capital in 1914. They were stationed in twelve of the surrounding forts, and manned the artillery and searchlights. The CRP had only twenty searchlights in late 1914; their number was doubled within a year, including mobile units, but it then saw no notable increase until 1918.

(**Opposite, above**) Frépillon (Val d'Oise), August 1915. The guns at the Frépillon post are simply conventional 75mm field guns set to fire at a high angle. They are placed here on wooden platforms, which were gradually replaced by metal patterns derived from fortress equipment. In the background, officers scour the skies using binoculars and a stereoscopic range-finder. When 64th Artillery took command of the capital's anti-aircraft artillery in September 1917, it consisted of fifty-three positions, each comprising two guns, two or three listening posts and a searchlight.

(**Opposite, below**) Eiffel Tower, Paris, July 1915. These Saint-Étienne guns are positioned on the tower's second level. As a key element in the military wireless network, the tower was protected by a number of machine guns, as well as several 37mm cannon. The weapons, however, made little real contribution to the capital's defence.

(**Above**) Compiègne (Oise), 17 March 1917. Pictured (left, foreground) is part of the wreckage of Zeppelin L39 (Kapitänleutnant Robert Koch). The airship had just raided England, dropping several bombs on the Kent coast. Caught by a gale, and possibly suffering an engine fault, it crossed the French coast near Dieppe (Seine-Maritime) at 3.55am. After battling south-eastwards towards Beauvais (Oise), the balloon started drifting again, and as dawn rose it was caught by AA fire over Compiègne. The French defences fired over 100 rounds before the Zeppelin caught fire and exploded – one fragment fell in gardens near the junction of Boulevard Gambetta and Rue de Paris. All seventeen crew members were killed.

(**Opposite, above**) Le Bourget (Seine-Saint-Denis), 31 July 1915. Illuminated by a searchlight, a Farman prepares for take-off. The call was a false alarm: no raid took place that night. By September 1915, the CRP could deploy fifteen Farmans, seven Caudrons and seventeen Voisins – armed with only twelve machine guns and twenty-four automatic rifles between them – plus eighteen Nieuports. Nor did any of these types possess the speed required. Even when the early warning system worked well, the outer line of listening posts gave only thirty-five minutes' notice of an attack, while a Farman needed forty minutes to reach its operational height of 4,000m.

(**Opposite, below**) Le Bourget (Seine-Saint-Denis), 30 May 1916. This line-up of Nieuports, the 10 (rear) and the 11 (foreground), represent the more up-to-date aircraft serving with the CRP. They belong to squadron N95, renumbered N395 that summer, and N461 in 1917. By the summer of 1918, the CRP could deploy 165 machines of all types, but no amount of pleading could rid it of its obsolete Farmans, some of which had to soldier on until the end of the war.

Paris, 1 February 1918. Many pilots struggled to find their home airfield while operating over the darkened city. Flying a Voisin bearing an owl badge on its nose, Maréchal des logis Jean Sachot (VC468) has spotted a likely open space and crashed on the Place de la Concorde. Both Sachot and his observer, Quartier-maitre Yves Le Juge, were badly injured. The night of 30–31 January 1918 had seen the first 'Gotha' raid, when eleven enemy aircraft – including one machine shot down by AA fire over Chelles (Seine-et-Marne) – dropped seventy bombs on the city and its suburbs.

Bois de Corbie, Beaumont-en-Beine (Aisne). French soldiers investigate the remains of the emplacement of one of the two Paris guns. This wood was the fourth site used, construction starting in April 1918. Masked by the German Operation Blücher offensive, the gun began firing on 27 May. Fifteen rounds were unleashed that day, but just seven were reported in Paris, with only one hitting a military target (a remount depot). The position remained in action until 9 August 1918, when advancing Allied troops forced the Germans out.

Chapter Six

Fit for service

The factional strife that so bedevilled the early years of French military aviation did not end with the war. Soldiers, airmen, manufacturers, press and politicians continued to battle for control, influencing the development of strategy, tactics – and machines. In August 1914, the French aircraft industry was the biggest in the world, and the government its major customer, but it remained a diverse, small-scale affair. With nineteen different types in use, from a dozen different manufacturers, all badly disrupted by the outbreak of war – skilled craftsmen called up, key iron-, steel- and textile-producing regions under enemy occupation, factories evacuated from Paris to the provinces – the service struggled initially to supply its front-line units. To stimulate production and to simplify maintenance and training, the director of aviation, General Hirschauer, decided to focus on a small number of types ordered in quantity, increasing monthly output by almost 50 per cent between January and August 1915. But the politicians were by now flexing their muscles, and in September 1915 Hirschauer was sacked, his staff post abolished, and Senator René Besnard appointed to a new ministerial role of under-secretary of state for aeronautics.

The energetic Besnard set to work immediately, returning specialist craftsmen to their employers, militarizing the flying schools, and supplementing the existing Service des Fabrications de l'Aviation (SFA), which placed contracts and supervised manufacture, with a new research and development arm, the Service Technique de l'Aéronautique (STAé). Besnard knew that modern production techniques and innovative design would be vital in achieving air superiority; yet lacking any powers of coercion, his hands were tied. Heedless of patriotic sentiment, and protected by lucrative deals for a fixed number of aircraft, contracted suppliers were reluctant to invest. Rather than develop new machines, they preferred the cheaper option of making incremental changes to existing types, in the process tying the air service to essentially obsolete machines long after rival manufacturers – and the enemy – had moved on.

By the autumn of 1915, the situation had reached crisis point. Press, politicians and heavy bomber manufacturers Breguet, Michelin and Voisin were demanding long-distance raids on targets in Germany, but serving airmen disagreed. The French co-operation machines were in desperate need of replacement: all were outdated, under-powered pushers, completely unprotected against attack from the rear.

Improved reconnaissance types and more tactical bombers were the military priorities. 'Our paramount objective is winning the land battle,' argued one officer. 'If we lose that, there is little point in bombing Cologne.' Besnard supported front-line opinion, attracting vitriolic criticism from the disappointed bombing lobby, and in February 1916 he was forced to resign. His post was abolished, and the service was returned to military control in the shape of Colonel Henry Régnier, an artilleryman who – like his predecessor Bernard – viewed aircraft as little more than an adjunct to the guns. Major Barès, the GQG aviation commander, had worked well with Besnard, but his relationship with Régnier quickly deteriorated, and only the untimely death of Charles de Rose in May 1916 saved him from the sack.

With politicians and press sniping relentlessly from the sidelines, the crisis of materiel gathered pace over the next few months. The Breguet-Michelins, Capronis, Farmans and Voisins of the bomber squadrons lacked the power and armament needed for long-range, large-scale daylight raids, and competitions organized in 1915 and 1916 failed to produce any viable new types. The cooperation squadrons were littered with antiquated machines: the new Nieuport 12 was judged difficult to fly, and even harder to land, while the new Caudron G.6 and R.4 three-seaters were only just starting to reach the front line. In despair at the aviation industry, the STAé was instructed to start designing new aircraft, while several Sopwith 1½ Strutters were purchased from the British as a stop-gap, redesignated the 1A.2, and then manu-factured under licence. Meanwhile the fighters so successful in the spring and summer of 1916 had been outclassed by new enemy types. Introduced late in the year, the Nieuport 17 was no match for the German Albatros D.II and D.III; its more powerful stablemates, the Nieuport 24, 24bis and 27, were not yet in production; and the superior SPAD 7 – delayed by engine problems and lack of production capacity – was yet to reach the squadrons in any quantity. By February 1917, only 268 SPADs had been received in total, and just 70 in the front line. In vain, Barès appealed to Michelin to build SPADs in place of its much-despised Breguet-Michelin bomber. André Michelin went straight to the prime minister, receiving permission to produce another 100 examples of a type condemned by Barès as 'undoubtedly one of the worst machines ever acquired by the service'.

In February 1917 Barès was dismissed, and in March a change of government restored the service to political control, with a new under-secretary, Daniel Vincent. At the same time, several new bomber and cooperation types were arriving on the airfields, the majority flattering to deceive. The Sopwith 1A.2 was obsolete by the time it entered service; the Voisin 8 bomber remained defenceless against the German fighters, while the Paul Schmitt 7 – designed in 1915 but delayed in pro-duction – proved a complete and costly failure. GQG begged Vincent to halt produc-tion of the Sopwith in favour of the superior new Breguet 14, but to no avail: long contracts left him powerless. Nor were the STAé-designed types any more effective:

the A.R.2 was little better than its Farman predecessors, while the outsize Letord caused severe overcrowding on the airfields.

In May 1917, the catastrophe on the Chemin des Dames brought a new commander-in-chief, General Philippe Pétain, and with him new operational ideas. Grand general offensives would be replaced by limited actions launched only after achieving sudden, overwhelming local superiority in firepower – and control of the air would be key to their success. In implementing his strategy, Pétain was aided by two significant appointments: in August 1917, Colonel Charles Duval became GQG aviation commander, and in September Jacques-Louis Dumesnil, recently an observer with C13, succeeded Daniel Vincent as under-secretary. In November, a further level of bureaucracy was added to the procurement process when responsibility for the SFA was transferred to munitions minister Louis Loucheur; yet somehow the personalities involved contrived to make the system work. By the spring of 1918, the trio had substantially increased aircraft production, using sub-contractors to manufacture just half-a-dozen types, among them several important new designs: the powerful and manouevrable SPAD 13 for the fighter squadrons; the stable yet agile Breguet 14B2 for the day bomber squadrons; the Voisin 10, and later the Farman F.50, for the night bombers. The Caudron R.11 long-range fighter replaced the Letord as a bomber escort, while the reconnaissance squadrons would receive the Breguet 14 or the new Salmson 2A.2.

In a time of rapid technological change, producing the right planes, in the right numbers, at the right time was no easy task. After each advance some new requirement arose, while the delay between an aircraft emerging in prototype, entering production, and arriving in the front line was always sufficient for an improved enemy design to appear, superseding its predecessor. Yet by November 1918, a massive state-sponsored mobilization had transformed the embryonic aviation sector. Now worth some 5 million francs, equivalent to almost 13 per cent of pre-war national output, and employing 183,000 people, almost a quarter of them women, the industry was vital not only to France, but also to the wider Allied war effort. Over the course of the conflict, some 52,000 aircraft were produced, in 365 different types, including 10,000 airframes and 25,000 engines despatched to the United States, Britain, Russia, Italy, Belgium and Romania.

(**Opposite, above**) Dieue-sur-Meuse (Meuse), 14 March 1916. French commander-in-chief, General Joseph Joffre (1852–1931), confers with his aviation commander, Major Édouard Barès (1872–1954). Appointed shortly after the outbreak of war, Barès (left) championed Charles de Rose, the SPAD 7 fighter and the need for more and better cooperation types, consequently drawing fire from bomber manufacturers and other entrenched interests. Sacked in February 1917, he served out the war with the infantry, his knowledge and expertise lost to the aviation service. But when the Armée de l'Air was established as an independent force in 1934, Barès became its first chief of staff.

(**Opposite, below**) René Besnard (1879–1952). The under-secretary appears somewhat ill-at-ease among a group of trainee pilots sporting an extraordinary variety of flying gear. A moderate leftist deputy for the Indre-et-Loire, Besnard had briefly occupied a number of ministerial posts before leaving for the front in 1914: 'Young, dedicated and affable, he had all the qualities required to succeed in his difficult task, particularly that of reconciling those two warring brothers, front and rear.' By supporting Barès, Besnard became a target of the bombing lobby, and he was dismissed in February 1916. He served in other wartime government posts before entering the senate in 1920.

(**Above left**) André Michelin (1853–1931). André Michelin and his brother Édouard (1859–1940) were pre-war French industrialists, founders of the famous tyre company, and passionate advocates of aviation. On the outbreak of war, they lobbied fiercely for their Breguet-Michelin bomber. Its flawed design and underpowered Canton-Unné engine were not what the service required. Nonetheless, prompted by munitions minister Albert Thomas, some 200 examples were ordered, and in September 1915 formed into their own bomber *groupe*, BM1. The last BM squadron was not disbanded until May 1918.

(**Above right**) Daniel Vincent (1874–1946). A Radical deputy, and later senator, for the Nord, Vincent served as an observer with bomber squadron V116 before his appointment as under-secretary in March 1917. He ordered the STAé to stop designing aircraft and tried to increase commercial output by sub-contracting manufacture and streamlining production techniques. Like Besnard, he came under sustained attack in parliament, and a change of government in September 1917 brought his resignation and transfer to the education portfolio.

(**Above**) Pierre-Étienne Flandin (1889–1958). A centre-right deputy for the Yonne, Flandin gained his wings in 1912 and served with MF33 in 1914–15. Returning to politics, he became a leading light of the bombing lobby. A fleet of 750 bombers could obliterate Essen and the Ruhr basin, he suggested in 1915: 'they are in essence just very long-range guns … that allow us to strike at the heart of the enemy arms industry'. In 1917, he served on the committee responsible for integrating US military aviation into the wider Allied effort; he later drafted the civil aviation clauses in the treaty of Versailles and, as a minister in the 1920s, helped to foster French civil aviation. He held further senior positions during the following decade, culminating in a brief spell as prime minister under the Vichy régime.

(**Opposite, above**) Villacoublay (Yvelines), 25 June 1918. President Raymond Poincaré (1860–1934) and Under-secretary Jacques-Louis Dumesnil (1882–1956) visit the airfield. Poincaré (in homburg) and Dumesnil (bearded, with cane) are standing in front of a Morane-Saulnier AI. Designated MoS.27 (single gun) and MoS.29 (twin gun), the AI equipped MS156 and MS158 in 1918. Engine problems led to its rapid relegation to air combat training units, where its undoubted agility proved useful. In the background are a Nieuport monoplane, a British Sopwith Dolphin (then being trialled by the French) and a SPAD.

(**Opposite, below**) Louis Loucheur (1872–1931), Paris, May 1918. An industrialist invited to join the government of Aristide Briand, Loucheur served as under-secretary of state for munitions from December 1916, and as minister from September 1917. In this capacity, he rationalized and energized French production to provide the tanks, aircraft and guns required for victory. Here (second from right), he waits to welcome an American Labour Party delegation to the Citroën works. Among his companions is a senior artillery staff officer, General Gustave Payeur (1863–1954), while gesticulating is car manufacturer André Citroën (1878–1935).

Villacoublay (Yvelines), June 1916. Pilot Adrien Levasseur (1890–1969) lays down the law to his companions, perhaps discussing the Nieuport to the rear. Levasseur had learnt to fly before the war, taking part in seaplane races and early editions of the Schneider Trophy. He later served with N57, before joining Nieuport as a test pilot in November 1915. 'It was vital that no plane entered front-line service without first being thoroughly tested,' insisted Auguste Heiligenstein (MF5/44/C106/229). 'The missions were quite dangerous enough without the risk of an aircraft unfit for service breaking up in mid-air.'

(**Opposite, above**) Villacoublay (Yvelines), 1918. Mechanics put the finishing touches to a Ponnier M.1. Originally developed in 1915, the prototype was piloted by Charles Nungesser in a test flight in January 1916. Inherently unstable, the aircraft crashed, leaving Nungesser with a fractured jaw and two broken legs. Although the type was never adopted for operational use, a handful did reach training establishments. Others entered the Belgian Air Service, whose pilots – led by ace Willy Coppens (1892–1986) – refused point-blank to fly it.

(**Opposite, below**) Issy-les-Moulineaux (Hauts-de-Seine). The judges of the 1915 bomber competition – including (third left) foreign minister and future president Alexandre Millerand (1859–1943) – contemplate a Voisin Triplane. The Voisin was designed as a heavy bomber capable of smashing Essen, but even Joseph Frantz, a veteran test pilot and the first confirmed victor in air-to-air combat, could do nothing with it. In competition, it was revealed as a slow, heavy monster unable to defend itself, and like all its fellow entrants it was rejected for further development.

(**Above**) Issy-les-Moulineaux (Hauts-de-Seine), 7 August 1915. In the park outside the Voisin factory stands the single prototype of the Voisin O. The Type O and the single-fuselage Type M were built at the same time, but were pursued no further. Their undercarriage sat too low to the ground to allow safe clearance for the propeller.

(**Opposite, above**) Villacoublay (Yvelines), 20 January 1916. This prototype Breguet 11 Corsaire could accommodate three gunners: one in in each of its two wing-mounted engine nacelles, and a third behind the pilot. The type might have served as an escort, but instead it was entered into the 1916 bomber competition. With its wedge-shaped spats removed, it performed well; but like many of its fellow entrants, its size led to its rejection in favour of more conventionally configured types.

(**Opposite, below**) Esquennoy (Oise), 24 August 1916. Curious aircrew clamber over this prototype Morane-Saulnier S heavy day bomber, winner of the 1916 bomber competition. Esquennoy was an operational airfield (then home to C51), so the Morane may have been present for evaluation in field conditions. Barès placed an order for 300 of the type, subsequently reduced to 90 by parliament on grounds of cost. In disgust, Barès cancelled the order in favour of licence-built Italian Capronis, and the Morane never entered squadron service.

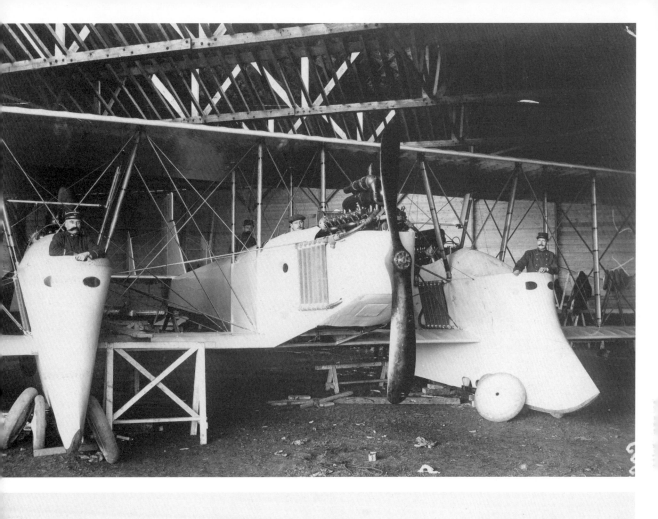

(**Opposite, above**) Villacoublay (Yvelines) 10 May 1918. The monstrous four-engined Blériot 71 was designed in 1917 to meet a specification for a strategic bomber capable of defending itself against enemy fighters. The only prototype was damaged at Villacoublay in an accident five days after this photograph was taken. The type was never selected for production and the wreck was scrapped.

(**Opposite, below**) Villacoublay (Yvelines), 30 May 1916. A prototype of the ungainly, unloved Salmson-Moineau S.M.1 stands on the airfield. In an attempt to reduce drag, the two engines were placed sideways in the fuselage and connected to the propellers by a complex set of gears. Worse still, the exhaust from the engines blew straight into the pilot's face. By mid-1917, thirty-two machines were serving with eleven different army cooperation squadrons. After suffering numerous accidents and mechanical problems, most were subsequently withdrawn, although some soldiered on until late 1918.

(**Above**) Boulogne-Billancourt (Hauts-de-Seine), 8 August 1918. Breguet 14 bombers roll through the production line at the Renault factory. The engines have been installed; now the fuselages await their canvas covering. By November 1918, 805 machines of this type were serving with seventy-three squadrons, bomber and army cooperation. The type also served with the US and Italian air services during the war. It was finally withdrawn from French service in the late 1920s.

(**Above**) Villacoublay (Yvelines), 9 July 1918. The wings of the Breguet 14 are mounted and rigged in the final assembly shop at the Breguet works. Presciently, in January 1914 Louis Breguet had moved his main plant to Villacoublay from Douai-La Brayelle (Nord). By 1918, the factory was turning out four Breguet 14s a day, and by the armistice a total of 2,000 had been built, either here or by sub-contractors. Douai, meanwhile, had suffered four years under German occupation.

(**Opposite, above**) Boulogne-Billancourt (Hauts-de-Seine), 8 July 1918. 'Should the women in our factories down tools for twenty minutes,' proclaimed General Joffre, 'the Allies will lose the war'. Here, at the Renault factory, women work on the Breguet 14, adding canvas to sections of wing. In January 1914, Renault had employed 190 women, forming 3.8 per cent of its workforce; by the spring of 1918, that number had soared to 6,770, or 31.6 per cent of the workforce.

(**Opposite, below**) Le Bourget (Seine-Saint-Denis), 1916. Planes in the General Aviation Reserve – Réserve Générale d'Aviation (RGA) – are captured in this aerial view. The RGA was responsible for despatching new aircraft to operational units. Pilots like Jean Navarre, however, thought nothing of flouting bureaucratic procedure, arriving unannounced to demand a new machine, then flying it back to base. The Le Bourget airfield was first planned in 1910, but work only began in 1915, when it was designated the main base for the Paris defences. Between the wars, it became the city's main airport, and it is now home to the Musée de l'Air et de l'Espace.

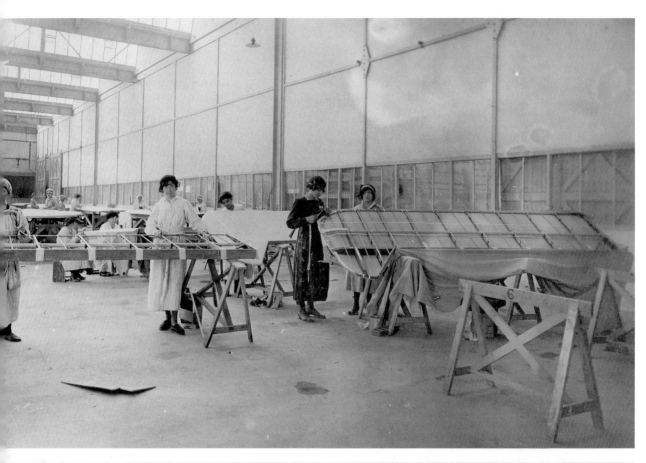

(**Above**) Saint-Cyr-l'École (Yvelines), February 1916. Clerks and mechanics are pictured in the spare parts stores at the aviation repair workshop – Atelier de Réparations d'Aviation (ARA). Among the materiel visible on the shelves are wheels, tyres and seats. Saint-Cyr was home to the Zodiac dirigible factory and a principal depot of the balloon service. A repair establishment for balloons and aircraft was also set up, with an eventual workforce of 4,000, many of them women.

(**Opposite**) Saint-Cyr-l'École (Yvelines), February 1916. A newly repaired aircraft is crated up to be returned to its squadron. The practice of sending all seriously damaged aircraft to the RGA for repair introduced intolerable delays, since the machines required virtual disassembly before they could be moved. To accelerate matters, a central aircraft park – Grand Parc Aéronautique (GPAé) – was established in May 1917, at Matouges (Marne), closer to the front line. Controlled by GQG, it undertook major repairs; light repairs were completed by the army aircraft parks.

Faverolles-et-Coëmy (Marne), April 1917. Aircraft damaged in accidents await assessment at this aviation park; they will either be repaired on site, sent to the ARA or GPAé, or scrapped. Every army, *escadre*, bomber *groupe* or fighter *groupe* included an aircraft park. Most of these fragments appear to come from Nieuports, but the wings (right) bear the winged snail badge of Heavy Artillery Flight 210. The squadron was then spotting for Fifth Army's heavy artillery over the Chemin des Dames, operating a diverse mixture of Caudron R.4s, Sopwiths and Letords, while also retaining a Nieuport 14 and a Morane Parasol as hacks.

Chapter Seven

On to victory

By March 1918, an enormous industrial effort had doubled the number of bomber and fighter squadrons. GQG aviation commander Charles Duval now had the means to create a powerful air reserve for use 'en masse', supporting Pétain's plans for limited attacks backed by overwhelming firepower. First, Duval reorganized the fighter and bomber *groupes* into larger *Escadres de Combat* and *Escadres de Bombardement*, placed under the direct orders of GQG; then he acted again, combining the fighter *groupes* and the day bombers – 585 machines in total – in two massive provisional mixed *groupements*, while placing the night bombers in two separate formations, each 100 machines strong. At the same time he allocated a number of fighter *groupes* directly to the armies, tasked solely with ensuring complete freedom of action for the cooperation squadrons over the front.

For Pétain and Duval alike, the needs of the infantry remained paramount. The battle would be won on the ground, they argued, so the ultimate purpose of aviation – directly or indirectly – was to support the land war. The bombers would target the enemy front lines to a depth of 20km, aiming for ammunition dumps, stations and important rail junctions. Meanwhile the fighters would seek out and destroy the enemy above and across the front lines – operating *en masse* or in mixed sorties as bomber escorts. The bombers would act as bait: unable to ignore them, the Germans would be drawn into combat and the fighters would pounce. New airfields would be constructed to turn the air reserve into a truly mobile offensive force, while French pilots were reminded of the need for flexibility – reconnaissance crews must be prepared for combat; fighters, to identify valuable intelligence.

To counter the expected German Spring offensive, the two *groupements* and one night bomber *groupe* were temporarily allocated to the Northern Army Group. The enemy attacked on 21 March 1918, using their aircraft in close support of the infantry and achieving notable early gains, but the French responded at once. Moving by night along the threatened front, and committing dozens of planes to the skies at a time, the squadrons swiftly acquired air superiority over the entire Picardy front, using air power to stall the Germans and relieve threatened Amiens. Formations up to eighty strong struck the enemy rear, disrupting supply lines and halting the advance of reinforcements, and by early April the offensive was running out of steam.

Although delighted by the performance of his air reserve, in mid-May Duval was experimenting again. The two mixed *groupements* were combined to create a single Air Division some 600 machines strong, and a fortnight later the new formation faced its first big test. On 27 May, the Germans renewed the offensive, making significant inroads into French positions with their opening attacks. The night bombers were immediately despatched to raid the German rear, and within forty-eight hours three *groupements* of Breguet 14 day bombers were attacking enemy columns ever deeper behind the lines, at times outstripping the effective range of their escorts. By the time the French counter-attacked on 11 June, 600 aircraft had been assembled to cover a 130km front.

Ever the pragmatist, Duval was prepared to adapt his formations to the evolving situation, and on 15 June he divided the Air Division into two Mixed Brigades – each composed of one *Escadre de Combat* and one *Escadre de Bombardement* – plus a specialist, two-squadron-strong photo-reconnaissance unit. Earlier photo-reconnaissance missions had crossed no deeper than 25km into enemy territory, but trials had shown the Breguet 14 capable of venturing much further. Stripped of all surplus weight, including armament, and carrying oxygen equipment and heated clothing for the crew, the type could operate at altitudes of 6,400m to 6,700m and penetrate up to 120km behind the lines. The Breguet did its work and got out fast: the prints were developed on the airfield, then passed to a team of interpreters who compiled a daily list of changes for the overall situation map. The robust, well-armed Salmson 2A.2 also operated across the German lines in groups of three or four: one photographic machine accompanied by two or three escorts from the same squadron.

Throughout August and September, the Mixed Brigades continued their attacks. The orders for the Allied counter-offensive had authorized the fighter and bomber *groupes* to harass the retreating Germans, licensing an all-out assault as soon as enemy troops were clearly identified. Ideally, the day bomber squadrons would receive dual protection: top cover from the SPADs – limited in range, but faster and more manoeuvrable than the enemy fighters – with close support from the heavily armed Caudron R.11s, which had the range to accompany the bombers all the way to the target. In practice, however, the R.11 entered full service more slowly than expected, with only six squadrons formed by November 1918, so the Breguets were often left to fend for themselves.

The Air Division had proved a powerful weapon in these closing months of war, capable of decisive intervention in the land battle; indeed, Pétain was planning a second division for his operations in Lorraine in 1919. Yet Duval faced a constant struggle to keep his squadrons together before renewed demands for strategic bombing and reprisal raids. In June, he refused to divert precious resources away from the ground by joining the British Independent Force formed to bomb German cities. In September, however, he gave way. The Mixed Brigades were disbanded, to be replaced by specialist bomber and fighter brigades, and that autumn the French were planning to participate in a projected joint bombing formation under the direct orders of the supreme Allied commander, Marshal Ferdinand Foch.

The last confirmed victory recorded by a French fighter came on 4 November 1918, during a patrol over Reims (Marne), when Sous-lieutenant Jean Morvan, Lieutenant James Connolly and Lieutenant Cook (SPA163) surprised a flight of four Fokkers, downing two. But the last confirmed victory of all came the following day – the work not of a pilot, but a gunner, Sergeant Pierre Raveneau (SAL277), who shot down one confirmed (and one unconfirmed) enemy aircraft over the Vosges. The unfortunate German was probably Sergeant Gustav Albrecht (Jasta 64w).

In the post-war period, the air service continued to form an integral part of the army, operating in support of land war objectives. 'In practice, the air service has to work in conjunction with the armies,' stated Colonel Duval. 'It would be impossible to grant it complete independence.' For the bomber enthusiasts, this hampered development; yet the army and navy resisted all plans for a third force until 1934, when the Armée de l'Air at last saw light of day. Fittingly, its first commander, in the last three months before his retirement, was General Édouard Barès – such a key figure in the wartime development of the air service, and for so long the advocate of an independent force.

(**Opposite, above**) Le Plessis-Belleville (Oise), 1 September 1918. General Charles Duval (1869–1958) arrives at a medals ceremony. Duval (centre) is flanked by several of his senior aviation commanders: (left) Majors Victor Ménard (1881–1954), Eugène Rocard (1880–1918) and Joseph Vuillemin (1883–1963); (right) Majors Édouard Duseigneur (1882–1940) and Philippe Féquant (1883–1938). Féquant (EC2), brother of pioneer aviator Albert, and Ménard (EC1) were pre-war pilots; Rocard (GB3), Vuillemin (EB12) and Duseigneur (GC11) had transferred to aviation during the conflict. Rocard, the grandfather of French prime minister Michel Rocard (1930–2016), was shot down eleven days later in a raid on the Saint-Mihiel salient. His companions, however, remained in the service after the war; in 1940, as chief of staff of the Armée de l'Air, Vuillemin would shoulder much of the blame for its poor performance.

(**Opposite, below**) Hétomesnil (Oise), August 1918. The Storks of GC12 were fêted throughout the war. Here, standing (left to right) are Sous-lieutenant Henri Rabatel (1894–1973), Sous-lieutenant Pierre Schmitter (1897–?), Captain Xavier de Sevin (1894–1963), Lieutenant René Fonck (1894–1953), Sous-lieutenant Jacques Puget (1896–1935), Lieutenant Émile Letourneau (1893–?), Adjudant Marcel Castex and Sous-lieutenant Léon Thouzellier (1893–1919); seated are Sous-lieutenant Louis Coudouret (1896–1929), Lieutenant Joseph Batlle (1894–1990) and Lieutenant Jean Dombray (1890–?). Rabatel served with SPA3; Fonck, Schmitter, Thouzellier, Coudouret and Batlle with SPA103 (Batlle as CO); and de Sevin, Dombray, Puget, Letourneau and Castex with SPA26 (de Sevin as CO; Castex as medical officer).

(**Above**) Hétomesnil (Oise), May 1918. Sous-lieutenant Marcel Duret (1896–1928), Adjudant Adrien Mion (1896–1940) and Sous-lieutenant Pierre Pendariès (1894–?), all pilots with SPA67, are pictured with a SPAD 13. SPA67 joined the Storks in 1918, replacing SPA73. Pendariès (N69/SPA67) scored seven confirmed victories; Mion (C27/SPA67), three; and Duret (CRP/SPA67), two. All three men survived the war, Duret and Mion remaining in the air service. Duret died in a training accident in May 1928, while Mion, the 'squadron comedian' according to journalist René Chavagnes, was killed in 1940 in an enemy raid on the airbase at Châteauroux-La Martinerie (Indre); his home town of Saint-Brieuc (Côtes d'Armor) later named a street in his honour.

Villeneuve-sur-Verberie (Oise), April 1918. Lieutenant René Fonck (1894–1953) prepares for take-off. Fonck (C47/SPA103) was the leading French ace of the war, with seventy-five confirmed victories. 'Fonck ... was an assassin,' reckoned Paul Tarascon (N3/31/SPA62). 'He simply dived, hit his opponent, or brought him down within three or four rounds, then slipped away.' SPA103 marked its aircraft with a variant of GC12's distinctive stork badge; Fonck, however, also displayed the squadron's original red star insignia on the wings of his machine.

(**Above left**) Roland Garros (1888–1918). Captured in April 1915, Garros (MS23/SPA26) spent almost three years as a prisoner-of-war in several different locations. After several failed attempts to escape by tunnel, sea and air, he finally walked out of the Magdeburg camp disguised as a German officer, crossed the country and swam to freedom across the Dutch border. Despite poor health and poor eyesight, Garros insisted on returning to front-line action. He struggled to adapt to the new realities of aerial combat, but added four victories to his tally before his death in a dogfight over Vouziers (Ardennes) on 5 October 1918.

(**Above right**) Jean Bozon-Verduraz (1889–1942). Bozon-Verduraz (C11/N/SPA3/94) was a pre-war cavalryman who transferred to aviation as a pilot in August 1914. He joined the Storks in June 1917, when posted to N3, and on 11 September 1917 flew alongside Georges Guynemer on the ace's last patrol, losing sight of his companion in a dogfight. He ended the war in command of SPA94, with eleven confirmed victories.

(**Left**) Villeneuve-sur-Verberie (Oise), April 1918. Sergeant Frank Baylies (1895–1918) is well swaddled against the cold. The American Baylies (N73/SPA3) originally served as an ambulance driver in France and the Balkans. Rejected by the US air service on grounds of poor eyesight, he joined the French service in May 1917 – initially posted to N73, but transferred a month later to SPA3. He achieved twelve victories with the squadron before his death in action on 17 June 1918, shot down over Crèvecoeur-Lassigny (Oise), in combat with the aircraft of Jasta 19.

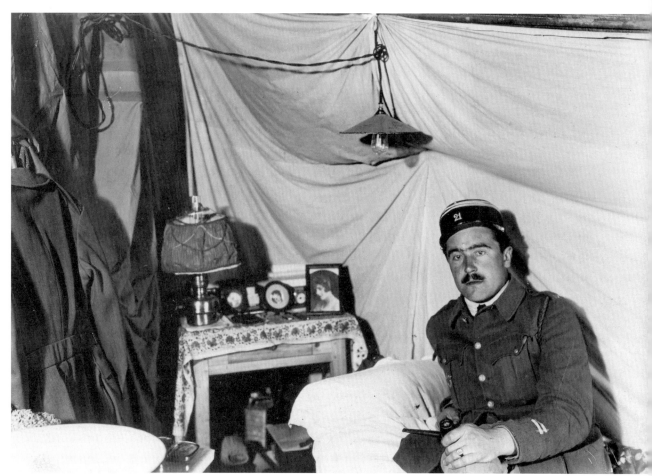

(**Above**) Hétomesnil (Oise), May 1918. Pictured here in his tent, Lieutenant Alfred Rougevin-Baville (1892–1982) still wears the kepi of 21st Dragoons, his regiment on the outbreak of war. Rougevin-Baville (N67/SPA99) earned his wings in early 1916 and was posted to N67. On 5 June 1918 he became CO of SPA99 (part of GC20): 'After all of eighteen months training … I found myself commanding a squadron composed mainly of chaps loath to follow me into action … I suffered some losses, looking on with sorrow while my lily-livered good-for-nothings got themselves killed.'

(**Opposite, above**) Mont-l'Évêque (Oise), 30 August 1918. Lieutenant Charles Nungesser, then serving with N65, dismounts from his SPAD 13. N65's squadron badge was a black dragon, but Nungesser retained his macabre skull-and-crossbones throughout the war. The name beneath the cockpit, 'Lt Verdier', was painted in honour of Nungesser's comrade, Lieutenant Louis Verdier-Fauvety (1886–1918), who had died of wounds two days earlier.

(**Opposite, below**) Le Plessis-Belleville (Oise), 30 August 1918. Lieutenant Marcel Émile Claude Haegelen (1896–1950) poses beside his SPAD 7. Haegelen (F8/N3/SPA100) transferred from the infantry, earning his wings in January 1916. He joined SPA100 on 11 March 1918 and stayed with the squadron until a week before the armistice. A noted balloon-buster, credited with twenty-three confirmed victories, he remained in the aviation service until 1929, when he became a test pilot with Hanriot. Re-enlisting in 1939, he was credited with a further victory in 1940. He later joined the Resistance, but was captured by the Germans in 1943 and imprisoned in Bourges.

(**Opposite**) Le Plessis-Belleville (Oise), 30 August 1918. Lieutenant Henri Hay de Slade (1893–1979) was appointed CO of SPA159 in July 1918, taking over a squadron demoralized by losses. The red stripes painted along the fuselage of his SPAD were added so his pilots could identify him in combat. He managed to restore morale, yet his squadron achieved only eleven victories under his leadership – eight to his credit and three to his second-in-command, Lieutenant Louis Risacher (1894–1986; SPA3/159).

(**Above**) Maurice Boyau (1888–1918). A former rugby international and captain of France, Boyau (N/SPA77) transferred to aviation from transport in 1915, earning his wings and serving initially as an instructor at Buc (Yvelines). He persisted in his demands for a front-line posting, and in October 1916 he was moved to N77, where he was credited with thirty-five confirmed victories (fourteen aircraft and twenty-one balloons). Immediately after his last victory, on 16 September 1918, he was shot down and killed by ground fire, flying to the aid of a comrade over Mars-la-Tour (Meurthe-et-Moselle).

(**Above left**) Lieutenant Léon Bourjade (1889–1924). A trainee priest in Switzerland at the outbreak of war, Bourjade (N/SPA152) initially joined the artillery. He transferred to aviation in 1917 and quickly established himself as a specialist 'balloon-buster', destroying twenty-seven balloons in his total of twenty-eight confirmed victories. Resuming his vocation after the war, he died while serving as a missionary in Papua.

(**Above right**) Sous-lieutenant Paul Waddington (1893–1986). A Frenchman of English extraction, Waddington (N67/N/SPA12/154/31) volunteered for aviation after his brother James was killed serving with VC116. Initially a motor driver with N67, he became a gunner with the squadron on 1 May 1916. After training at Buc and Avord, he gained his wings in January 1917, ending the war with twelve confirmed victories.

(**Opposite, above**) Baye (Marne), 27 July 1918. A SPAD 12 of SPA48 has its tail repaired. Then part of GC18, SPA48 remained at Baye for less than a month, supporting Allied counter-attacks on the Marne. First introduced in December 1916 by the CO, Captain Georges Matton (1888–1917), and Lieutenant Armand Galliot de Turenne (1891–1980), the squadron's bold cockerel badge is here much smeared by a trail from the engine exhaust. The badge was reproduced in this much larger form the following year. Matton (N57/48) achieved nine confirmed victories before being shot down in combat on 10 September 1917, over Keukelare (West-Vlaanderen) – one of four SPADs set upon by ten German single-seaters. Galliot de Turenne (N48/SPA12) recorded fifteen confirmed victories.

(**Opposite, below**) Trécon (Marne), July 1918. Aspirant Paul Honnorat (1894–?) and his regular observer Lieutenant Martin prepare for take-off in their Salmson 2A.2. Honnorat (SAL16) had arrived with the squadron in April 1918, one month after Martin. The squadron badge, a winged question mark, is just visible on the side of the fuselage. The Salmson 2A.2 was one of the best French aircraft of the war – robust, reliable, well-armed, easily maintained and capable of absorbing a fair amount of damage (although the distance between pilot and observer could cause communication difficulties). The availability of this reliable reconnaissance machine revolutionized French intelligence-gathering during the last year of the war.

(**Above**) Pretz-en-Argonne (Meuse), September 1918. A Salmson 2A.2 of SAL16 prepares for take-off. The 2A.2 was notably well armed, with a fixed machine gun fitted above the nose, and a twin machine gun for the observer. Although under the orders of Second Army, SAL16 spent brief periods under Italian or American control in late summer during the second battle of the Marne and the battle of Saint-Mihiel.

(**Opposite, above**) Villeneuve-lès-Vertus (Marne), December 1917. A Breguet 14 B.2 bomber of BR111 makes a low pass over the airfield. Clearly visible is the swan adopted by the squadron as its badge in 1917. Aft comes the personal insignia of the crew – a shield bearing stars and stripes suggesting an American connection.

(**Opposite, below**) Villeneuve-lès-Vertus (Marne), December 1917. A BR111 pilot takes the controls of his Breguet 14 bomber – the map, folded and attached to the cockpit, remains easily visible throughout. With its exceptional operational height and range, the Breguet 14 could also undertake long-range photo-reconnaissance missions. 'We began in groups of three, combining our firepower to deter the enemy fighters,' remembered Captain Paul-Louis Weiller (MF22/40/C21/BR224). 'We took some losses, but our six machine guns were enough to inflict some damage of their own, and we looked after ourselves pretty well. Shortage of materiel subsequently forced a change in tactics to one plane flying as high as possible. Taking photographs was our main objective, not getting into a scrap.'

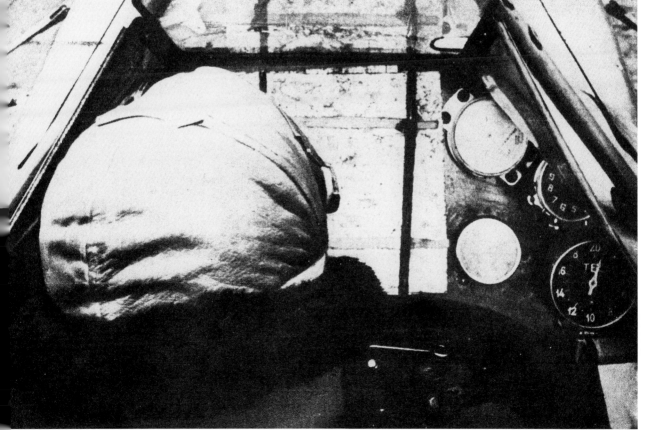

(**Above**) Roissy-en-France, 21 August 1918. Pilots and crew of BR128 and BR107 (the two squadrons comprising 2nd Brigade, GB3) are seen here at their base. Centre (with cane) is Captain René Le Forestier (1885–1963), CO of BR128. Le Forestier (VB103/PS127/BR111/128) had joined the squadron two months earlier: 'An excellent CO who through his bravery and coolness earned the trust of his unit and turned it into an elite squadron'. To his right (in the pale kepi) is his observer Lieutenant Louis Dauvin (1896–1969), who joined the squadron from the training school at Cazaux (Ariège) in November 1917. Le Forestier flew over forty bomber raids; Dauvin, fifty-seven.

(**Opposite, above**) Roissy-en-France, 20 August 1918. Sous-lieutenant Félix Brouet (left) and his gunner, Adjudant André Monard, are pictured with their Breguet 14. As part of BR128, the pair took part in eighty bombing operations and three espionage missions, and were also credited with shooting down three enemy aircraft. Monard's younger brother Henri was a pilot in the same squadron. The origin of the squadron's scarab beetle device is unknown.

(**Opposite, below**) Roissy-en-France, 21 August 1918. Adjudant-chef Paul Vanson, a veteran of seventy missions, and his gunner Adjudant François Suzanne (eighty missions) are seen in front of their Breguet 14. The winged serpent badge of their squadron, BR107, was introduced by Lieutenant Hubert de Geffrier (1893–1968), CO from June 1917 to September 1918. It was based on a device from his family coat-of-arms.

(**Above**) Roissy-en-France, 20 August 1918. Maréchal des logis Raymond Rousseau (left), a pilot and veteran of forty missions, and his gunner/photographer Adjudant Léon Pellard (twenty-six missions) are pictured in front of their Breguet 14. Rousseau was promoted to adjudant that same day. The badge of their squadron BR126 was a white diagonal band edged in red.

(**Opposite, above**) Poix (Somme), May 1918. This Caudron R.11, 14, was piloted by Adjudant Glenn Sitterly, one of six Americans then serving with C46. He was shot down in July, then transferred to single-seaters with SPA38, part of GC22. C46 was the first squadron to be equipped with the R.11; its former CO, Captain Didier Lecour-Grandmaison (1889–1917) had contributed to its design. Only six squadrons had been equipped with the type by November 1918, making its wartime contribution hard to assess. It certainly impressed contemporaries, as this style of 'battleplane' continued to serve into the 1930s.

(**Opposite, below**) Conflans-en-Jarnisy (Meurthe-et-Moselle). This aerial view looks north over this crucial – and frequently raided – railway junction, where lines from German-occupied Luxembourg met others running in many directions behind enemy lines. On 14 September 1918, the bombers of EB13 incurred heavy casualties raiding the target: BR131 lost six machines shot down, with one reported missing; BR132 lost four shot down, with four reported missing.

(**Above**) Villacoublay (Yvelines), 20 February 1918. A number of improved versions of the Voisin bomber were introduced over the course of the war. All proved unsuitable for daytime use and were relegated to night operations only. Here, an American Case tractor tows a Voisin 10 back to its hangar.

(**Opposite, above**) Valmy (Marne), September 1918. A Delahaye van of the army meteorological service – the Service Météorologique Militaire – takes its readings. From August 1914 onwards, the national weather service – the Bureau Centrale Météorologique – provided GQG with three forecasts a day. However, the huge increase in aerial activity, and a growing awareness of the impact of atmospheric conditions on the accuracy of long-range artillery, prompted the army to create its own service, which began operations in November 1916.

(**Opposite, below**) Near Méru (Oise), April 1918. A convoy of Packard lorries speeds its cargo of hangar frames to their destination. Pétain planned to keep the enemy off-balance by regularly switching the location and direction of attacks, requiring squadrons to move operating base quickly. Hangars and huts were easy to dismantle and re-erect. 'How far did I get describing our moves?' asked Raymond Montgolfier, as SAL39 ground crew tried to keep pace with the shifting front line. 'I can hardly remember what I said on my last card, Mother dear.'

Esplanade, Metz (Moselle), 19 November 1918. The war is over. Here, practically anonymous among the crowds, Charles Nungesser (centre, pale kepi) waits to witness General Pétain receiving his marshal's baton. Gilbert Sardier (N77/SPA48) had celebrated the armistice in Paris eight days earlier: 'we were wearing our medals, so a few people recognized us. The night was lively … more than lively!'